STUFF YOU NEED TO KNOW ABOUT THE HUMAN BODY

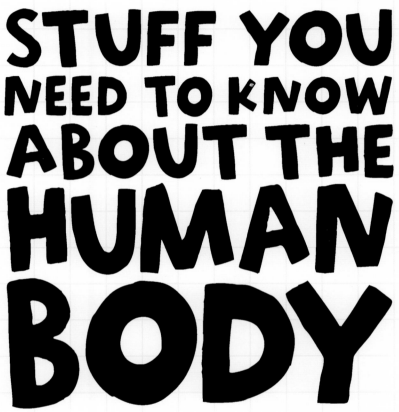

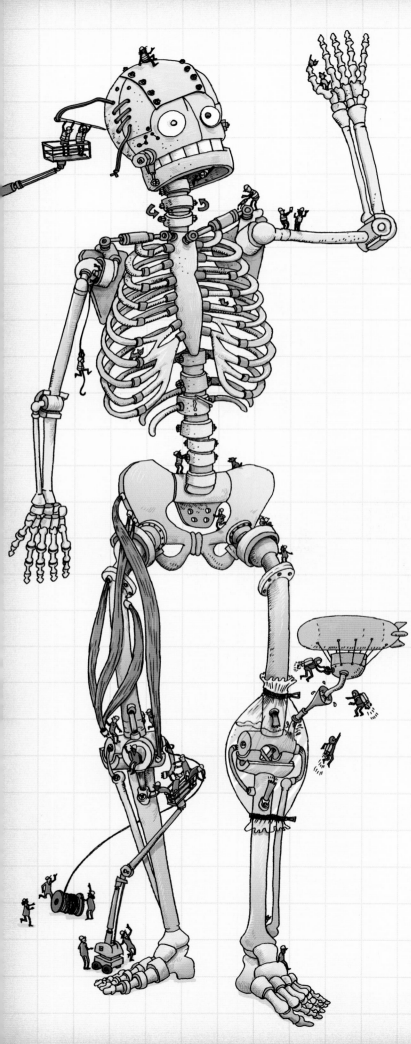

A FIREFLY BOOK

Published by Firefly Books Ltd. 2017

First printing

Publisher Cataloging-in-Publication Data (U.S.)

Names: Farndon, John, author. | Hutchinson, Tim, illustrator.
Title: Stuff You Need to Know About the Human Body / John
    Farndon, Tim Hutchinson.
Description: Richmond Hill, Ontario, Canada : Firefly Books, 2017.
    | Includes index. | Summary: "A fascinating introduction to the
    human body using large, colorful diagrams brought to life by
    tiny people performing the actions explained in the text" –
    Provided by publisher.
Identifiers: ISBN 978-1-77085-981-4 (paperback)
Subjects: Human body – Juvenile literature. |
    Human anatomy – Juvenile literature. |
    Human physiology – Juvenile literature. | BISAC: JUVENILE
    NONFICTION / Science & Nature / Anatomy & Physiology.
Classification: LCC QP37.F376 |DDC 612 – dc23

Library and Archives Canada Cataloguing in Publication

Farndon, John, author
        Stuff you need to know about the human body / John
Farndon ; Tim Hutchinson, illustrator.
Includes index.
ISBN 978-1-77085-981-4 (flexibound)
        1. Human body--Juvenile literature. 2. Human
anatomy--Juvenile literature. 3. Human physiology--Juvenile
literature. 4. Human biology--Juvenile literature. I. Hutchinson, Tim,
illustrator II. Title.
QP37.F37 2017   j612   C2017-900512-X

Published in the United States by
Firefly Books (U.S.) Inc.
P.O. Box 1338, Ellicott Station
Buffalo, New York 14205

Published in Canada by
Firefly Books Ltd.
50 Staples Avenue, Unit 1
Richmond Hill, Ontario L4B
0A7

Printed in China by 1010 Printing International Ltd

Conceived, edited and designed by
Marshall Editions
Part of The Quarto Group
First Published by
QED Publishing
Part of The Quarto Group
The Old Brewery, 6 Blundell Street
London N7 9BH, UK

Publisher: Maxime Boucknooghe
Editorial Director: Laura Knowles
Art Director: Susi Martin
Designed and Edited by Tall Tree Ltd

STUFF YOU NEED TO KNOW ABOUT THE HUMAN BODY

John Farndon

ILLUSTRATED BY
Tim Hutchinson

FIREFLY BOOKS

CONTENTS

* INDICATES A GATEFOLD SECTION

WELCOME TO YOUR BODY!

Bodies come in all shapes and sizes, but just what goes on inside? We've got a team of tiny tour guides to take you on an amazing roller-coaster journey around your body. Here are some of the weird places you'll be visiting...

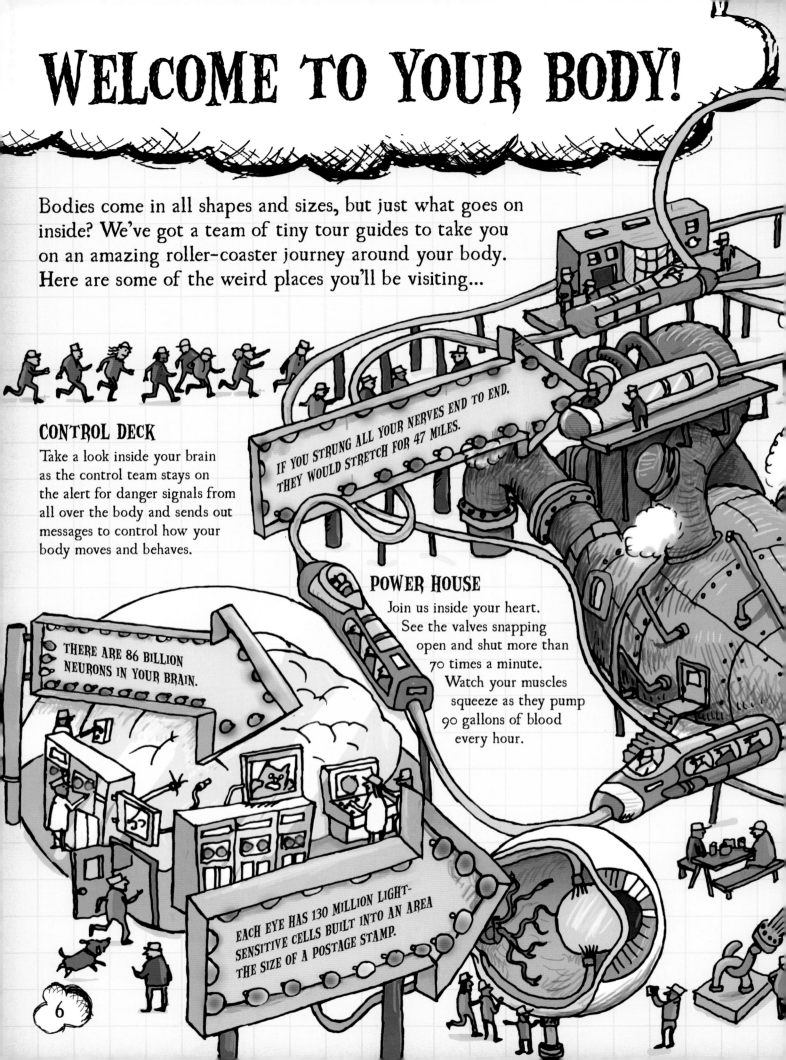

CONTROL DECK

Take a look inside your brain as the control team stays on the alert for danger signals from all over the body and sends out messages to control how your body moves and behaves.

IF YOU STRUNG ALL YOUR NERVES END TO END, THEY WOULD STRETCH FOR 47 MILES.

POWER HOUSE

Join us inside your heart. See the valves snapping open and shut more than 70 times a minute. Watch your muscles squeeze as they pump 90 gallons of blood every hour.

THERE ARE 86 BILLION NEURONS IN YOUR BRAIN.

EACH EYE HAS 130 MILLION LIGHT-SENSITIVE CELLS BUILT INTO AN AREA THE SIZE OF A POSTAGE STAMP.

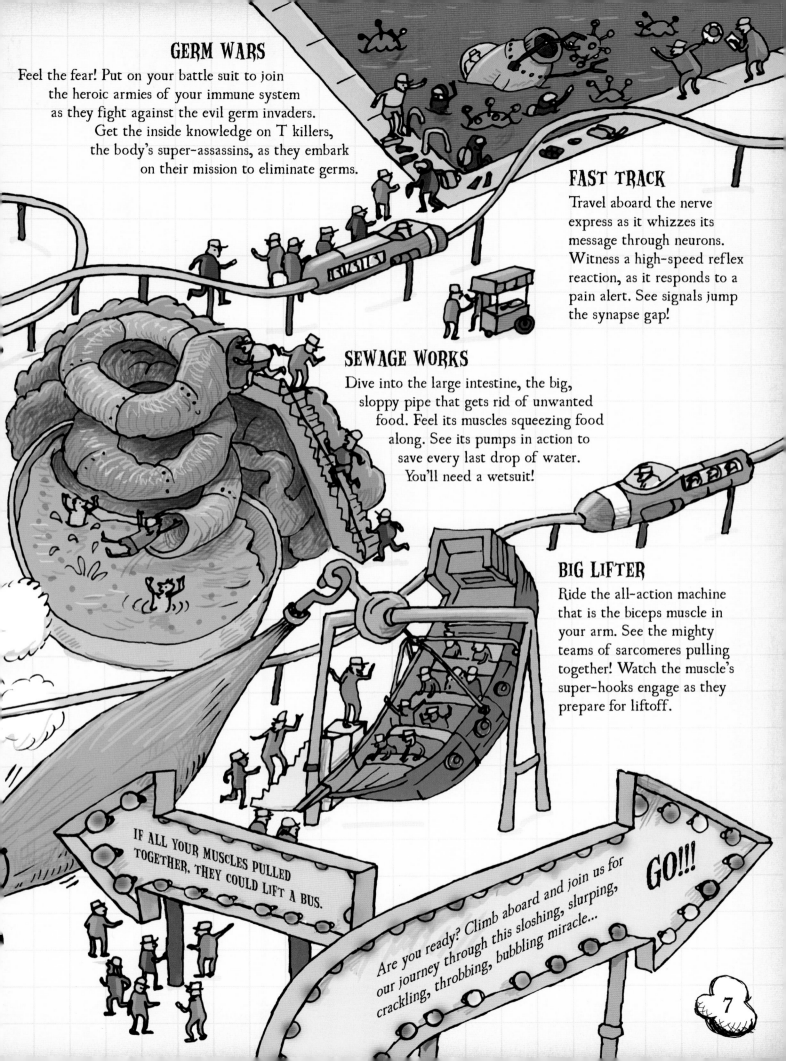

GERM WARS

Feel the fear! Put on your battle suit to join the heroic armies of your immune system as they fight against the evil germ invaders. Get the inside knowledge on T killers, the body's super-assassins, as they embark on their mission to eliminate germs.

FAST TRACK

Travel aboard the nerve express as it whizzes its message through neurons. Witness a high-speed reflex reaction, as it responds to a pain alert. See signals jump the synapse gap!

SEWAGE WORKS

Dive into the large intestine, the big, sloppy pipe that gets rid of unwanted food. Feel its muscles squeezing food along. See its pumps in action to save every last drop of water. You'll need a wetsuit!

BIG LIFTER

Ride the all-action machine that is the biceps muscle in your arm. See the mighty teams of sarcomeres pulling together! Watch the muscle's super-hooks engage as they prepare for liftoff.

IF ALL YOUR MUSCLES PULLED TOGETHER, THEY COULD LIFT A BUS.

Are you ready? Climb aboard and join us for our journey through this sloshing, slurping, crackling, throbbing, bubbling miracle... GO!!!

WHAT DO YOU NEED TO MAKE A BODY?

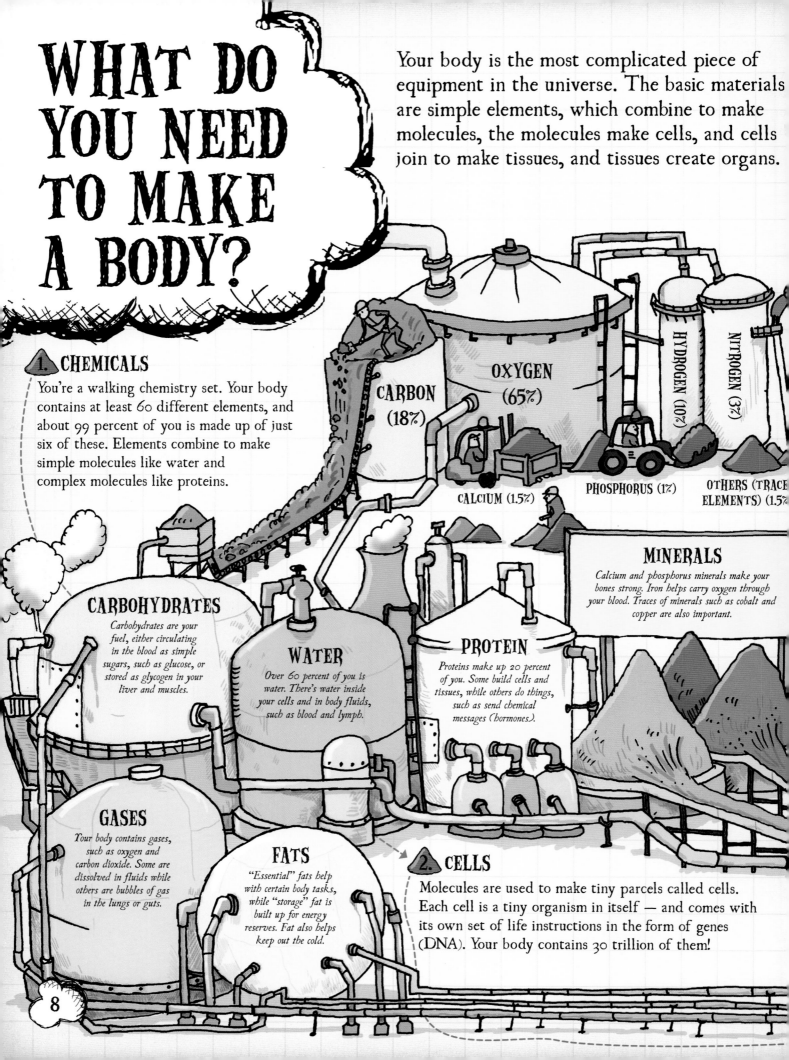

Your body is the most complicated piece of equipment in the universe. The basic materials are simple elements, which combine to make molecules, the molecules make cells, and cells join to make tissues, and tissues create organs.

1. CHEMICALS

You're a walking chemistry set. Your body contains at least 60 different elements, and about 99 percent of you is made up of just six of these. Elements combine to make simple molecules like water and complex molecules like proteins.

OXYGEN (65%)

CARBON (18%)

HYDROGEN (10%)

NITROGEN (3%)

CALCIUM (1.5%)

PHOSPHORUS (1%)

OTHERS (TRACE ELEMENTS) (1.5%)

MINERALS

Calcium and phosphorus minerals make your bones strong. Iron helps carry oxygen through your blood. Traces of minerals such as cobalt and copper are also important.

CARBOHYDRATES

Carbohydrates are your fuel, either circulating in the blood as simple sugars, such as glucose, or stored as glycogen in your liver and muscles.

WATER

Over 60 percent of you is water. There's water inside your cells and in body fluids, such as blood and lymph.

PROTEIN

Proteins make up 20 percent of you. Some build cells and tissues, while others do things, such as send chemical messages (hormones).

GASES

Your body contains gases, such as oxygen and carbon dioxide. Some are dissolved in fluids while others are bubbles of gas in the lungs or guts.

FATS

"Essential" fats help with certain body tasks, while "storage" fat is built up for energy reserves. Fat also helps keep out the cold.

2. CELLS

Molecules are used to make tiny parcels called cells. Each cell is a tiny organism in itself — and comes with its own set of life instructions in the form of genes (DNA). Your body contains 30 trillion of them!

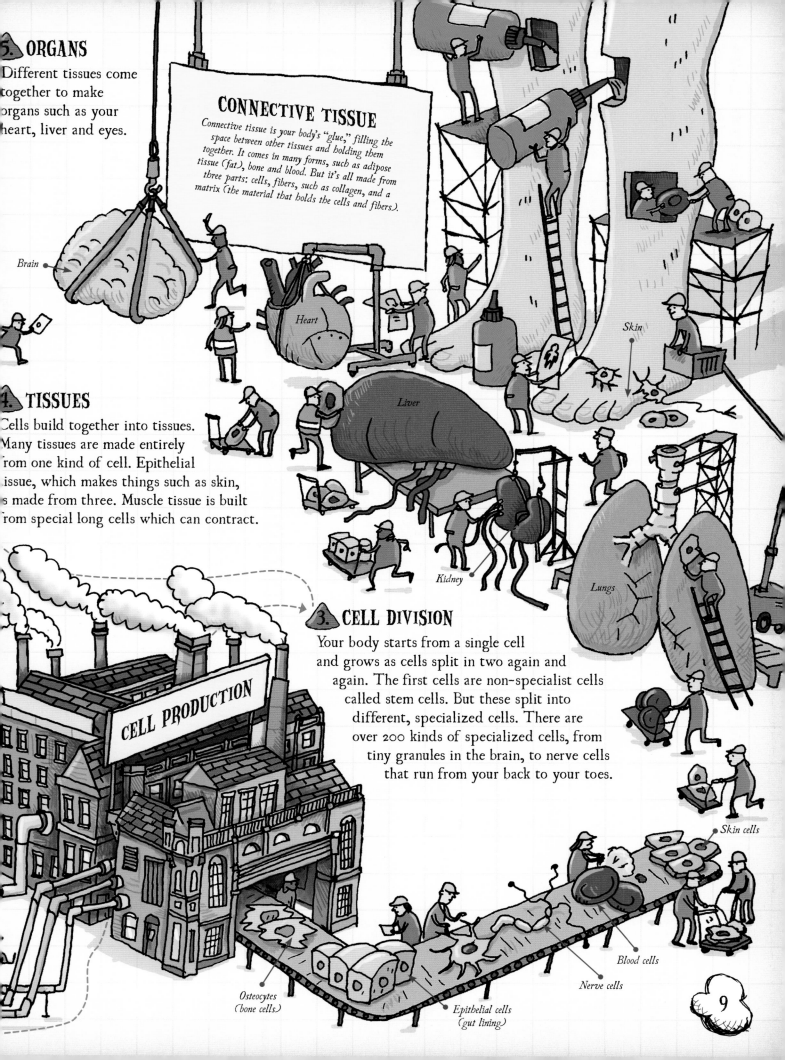

5. ORGANS

Different tissues come together to make organs such as your heart, liver and eyes.

CONNECTIVE TISSUE

Connective tissue is your body's "glue," filling the space between other tissues and holding them together. It comes in many forms, such as adipose tissue (fat), bone and blood. But it's all made from three parts: cells, fibers, such as collagen, and a matrix (the material that holds the cells and fibers).

Brain

Heart

Liver

Skin

4. TISSUES

Cells build together into tissues. Many tissues are made entirely from one kind of cell. Epithelial tissue, which makes things such as skin, is made from three. Muscle tissue is built from special long cells which can contract.

Kidney

Lungs

CELL PRODUCTION

3. CELL DIVISION

Your body starts from a single cell and grows as cells split in two again and again. The first cells are non-specialist cells called stem cells. But these split into different, specialized cells. There are over 200 kinds of specialized cells, from tiny granules in the brain, to nerve cells that run from your back to your toes.

Skin cells

Blood cells

Nerve cells

Osteocytes (bone cells)

Epithelial cells (gut lining)

WHAT GOES ON INSIDE A CELL?

Your body is made from trillions of cells so tiny you can only see them with a powerful microscope. Yet each cell is a chemical factory, always buzzing with activity.

THE FACTORY BUILDING

Every cell is enclosed by a thin wall or membrane, with tiny hatches that let the right chemicals in and out. The cell is held together by a framework or "cytoskeleton" of threads called microtubules. Inside, there's a jellylike fluid called cytoplasm — "cyto" means cell. Within the cytoplasm float tiny organs or "organelles," each with its own task.

NUCLEUS CONTROL

NUCLEOLUS

1. CONTROL CENTER

The nucleus is the control center. Here, all your body's programs for living are stored on strands of the chemical DNA. DNA is like a computer's memory. Each strand is a list of instructions for making the proteins to build a human body.

2. SENDING OUT INSTRUCTIONS

To keep going, the cell only needs a few proteins. So sections of DNA with the right instructions are copied onto a form of DNA called messenger RNA or mRNA. The copies are sent out to get the proteins made, while the DNA is kept safe.

mRNA

RER

3. FETCHING MATERIALS

At the same time, short pieces of RNA called transfer RNA or tRNA are at work. Each grabs one of the amino acids needed to build the protein.

Amino acids

tRNA

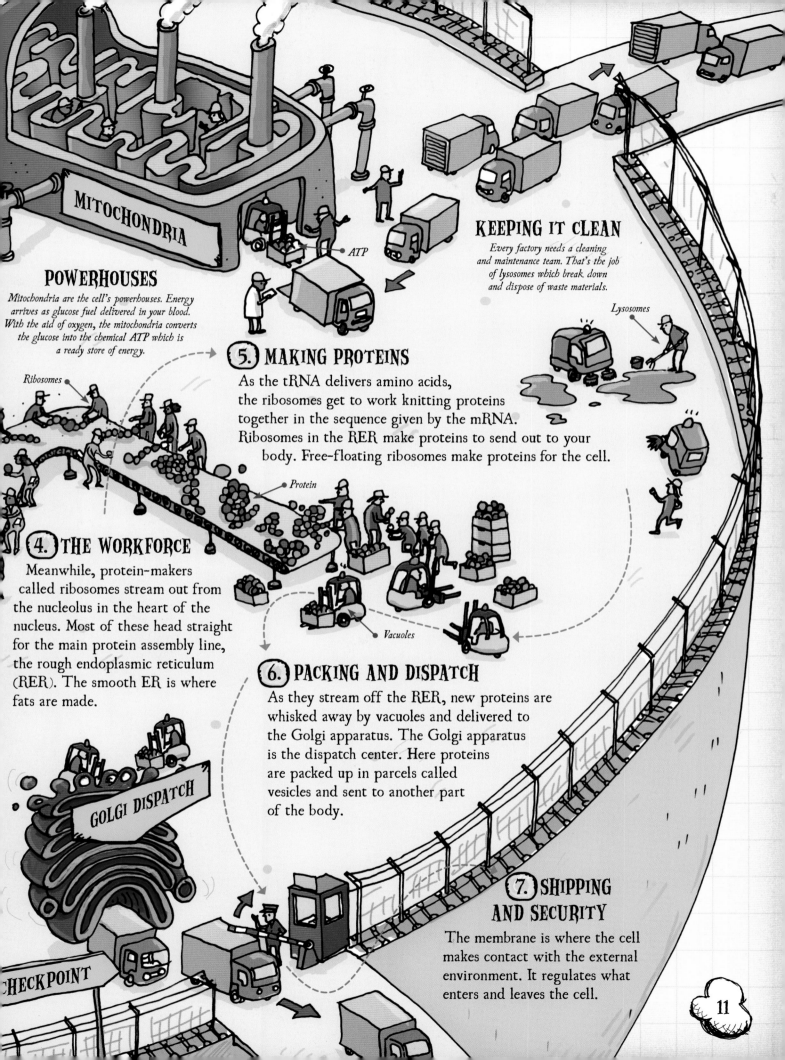

MITOCHONDRIA

POWERHOUSES

Mitochondria are the cell's powerhouses. Energy arrives as glucose fuel delivered in your blood. With the aid of oxygen, the mitochondria converts the glucose into the chemical ATP which is a ready store of energy.

Ribosomes

ATP

KEEPING IT CLEAN

Every factory needs a cleaning and maintenance team. That's the job of lysosomes which break down and dispose of waste materials.

Lysosomes

5. MAKING PROTEINS

As the tRNA delivers amino acids, the ribosomes get to work knitting proteins together in the sequence given by the mRNA. Ribosomes in the RER make proteins to send out to your body. Free-floating ribosomes make proteins for the cell.

Protein

4. THE WORKFORCE

Meanwhile, protein-makers called ribosomes stream out from the nucleolus in the heart of the nucleus. Most of these head straight for the main protein assembly line, the rough endoplasmic reticulum (RER). The smooth ER is where fats are made.

Vacuoles

6. PACKING AND DISPATCH

As they stream off the RER, new proteins are whisked away by vacuoles and delivered to the Golgi apparatus. The Golgi apparatus is the dispatch center. Here proteins are packed up in parcels called vesicles and sent to another part of the body.

GOLGI DISPATCH

CHECKPOINT

7. SHIPPING AND SECURITY

The membrane is where the cell makes contact with the external environment. It regulates what enters and leaves the cell.

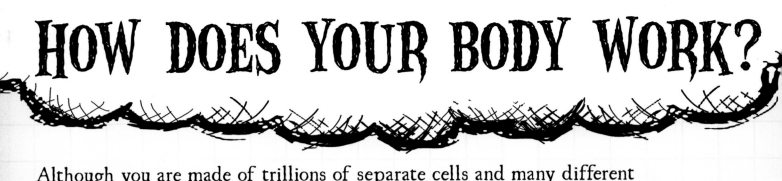

Although you are made of trillions of separate cells and many different organs, they all work together in systems. Some of these systems, such as the skeleton, extend throughout your body. Others are local, such as your urinary system, which controls your body's water content.

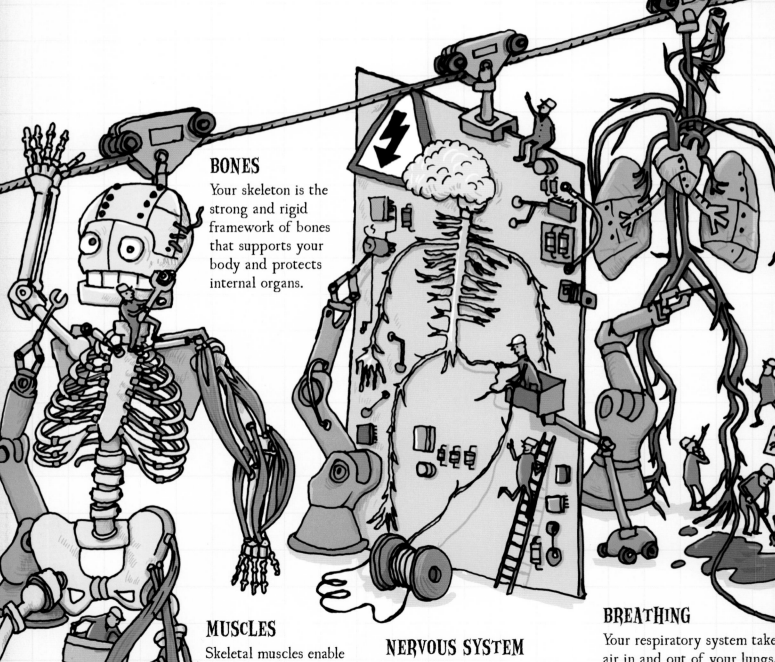

BONES
Your skeleton is the strong and rigid framework of bones that supports your body and protects internal organs.

MUSCLES
Skeletal muscles enable you to move. Other muscles control organs inside your body.

NERVOUS SYSTEM
This is your body's communication network and includes your brain, spinal cord and nerves.

BREATHING
Your respiratory system take air in and out of your lungs, delivering oxygen to the body, and getting rid of carbon dioxide.

12

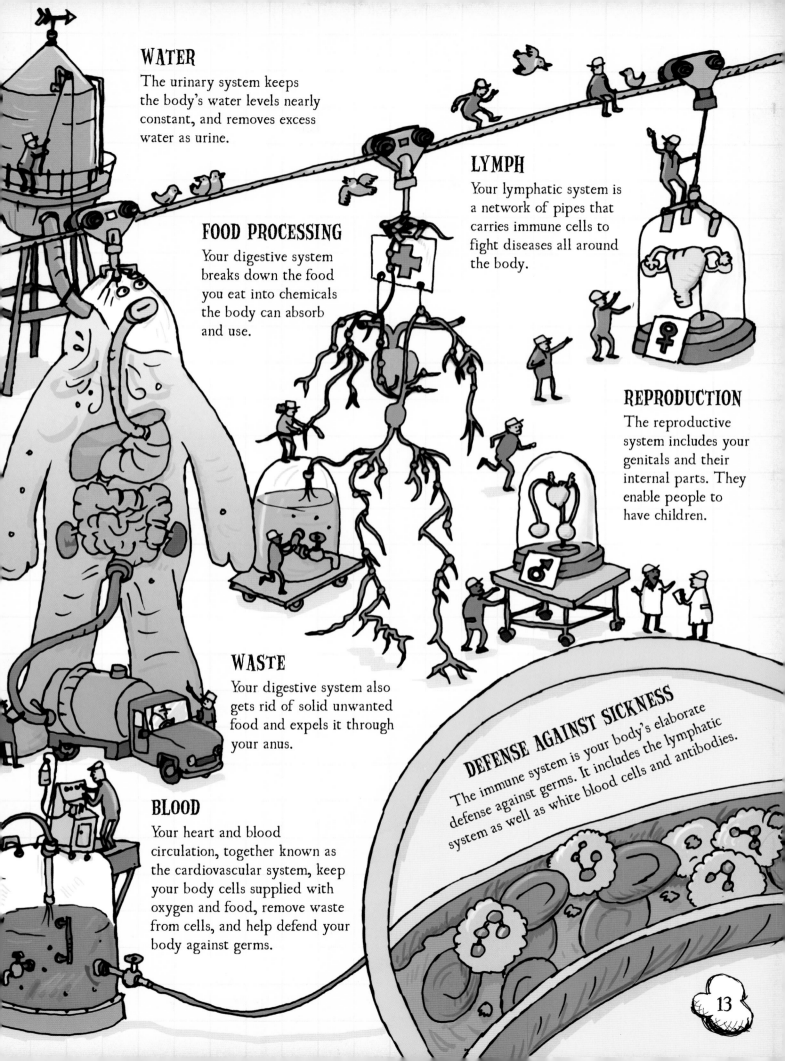

WATER

The urinary system keeps the body's water levels nearly constant, and removes excess water as urine.

LYMPH

Your lymphatic system is a network of pipes that carries immune cells to fight diseases all around the body.

FOOD PROCESSING

Your digestive system breaks down the food you eat into chemicals the body can absorb and use.

REPRODUCTION

The reproductive system includes your genitals and their internal parts. They enable people to have children.

WASTE

Your digestive system also gets rid of solid unwanted food and expels it through your anus.

DEFENSE AGAINST SICKNESS

The immune system is your body's elaborate defense against germs. It includes the lymphatic system as well as white blood cells and antibodies.

BLOOD

Your heart and blood circulation, together known as the cardiovascular system, keep your body cells supplied with oxygen and food, remove waste from cells, and help defend your body against germs.

13

HOW DO YOU BREATHE?

Your body cells need oxygen from air to produce energy. Without oxygen, cells die. That's why you breathe — to get oxygen from the air. If you stop breathing even for a few minutes, you will lose consciousness and soon die. Fortunately, your lungs are an amazing system for extracting lots of oxygen from the air every few seconds.

1. SWELLING YOUR CHEST

Breathing starts with your diaphragm. This is a sheet of muscle that domes up under your lungs. When you breathe in, it tightens and flattens, making more space for your lungs. At the same time, muscles between your ribs pull your chest outward and upward.

Ribs

2. SUCKING IN AIR

As your chest expands, it causes air to be sucked in through your mouth or nose. The air rushes down your windpipe, or trachea, until it reaches a fork inside your chest. Here the airways divide in two, with one branch, or "bronchus," leading to the left lung and one to the right. Your lungs fill up with air like balloons.

Diaphragm

14

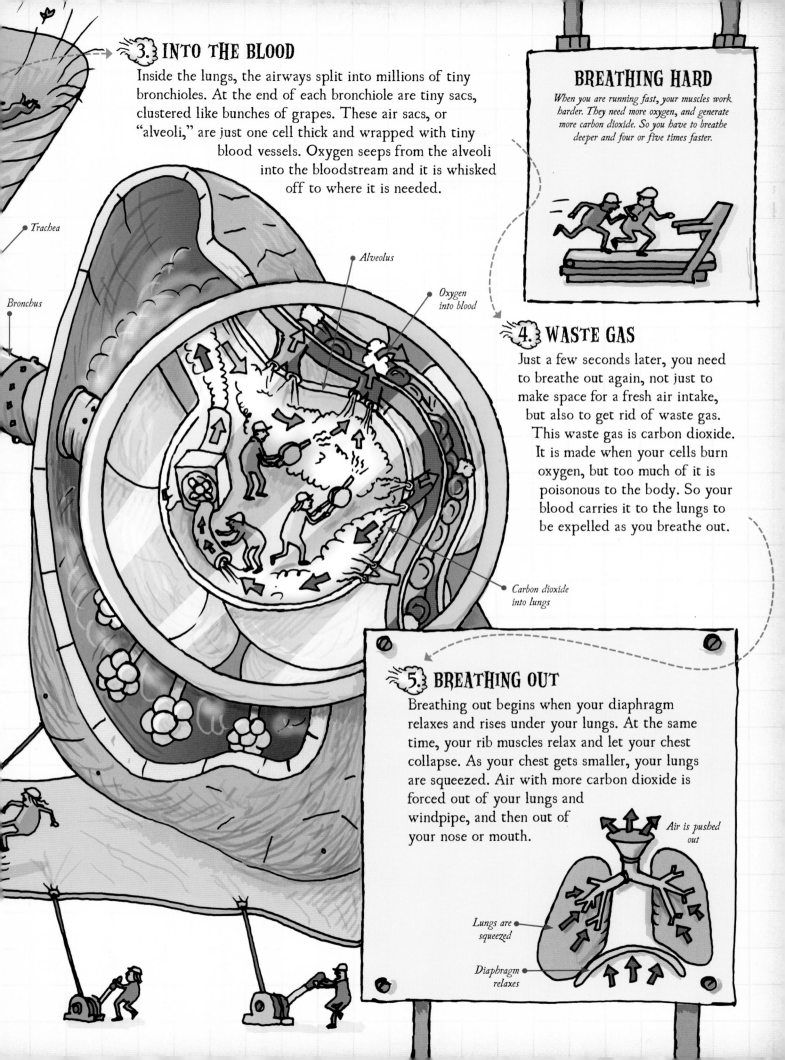

3. INTO THE BLOOD

Inside the lungs, the airways split into millions of tiny bronchioles. At the end of each bronchiole are tiny sacs, clustered like bunches of grapes. These air sacs, or "alveoli," are just one cell thick and wrapped with tiny blood vessels. Oxygen seeps from the alveoli into the bloodstream and it is whisked off to where it is needed.

Trachea

Bronchus

Alveolus

Oxygen into blood

Carbon dioxide into lungs

BREATHING HARD

When you are running fast, your muscles work harder. They need more oxygen, and generate more carbon dioxide. So you have to breathe deeper and four or five times faster.

4. WASTE GAS

Just a few seconds later, you need to breathe out again, not just to make space for a fresh air intake, but also to get rid of waste gas. This waste gas is carbon dioxide. It is made when your cells burn oxygen, but too much of it is poisonous to the body. So your blood carries it to the lungs to be expelled as you breathe out.

5. BREATHING OUT

Breathing out begins when your diaphragm relaxes and rises under your lungs. At the same time, your rib muscles relax and let your chest collapse. As your chest gets smaller, your lungs are squeezed. Air with more carbon dioxide is forced out of your lungs and windpipe, and then out of your nose or mouth.

Air is pushed out

Lungs are squeezed

Diaphragm relaxes

WHY IS YOUR BLOOD RED?

Blood is your body's transport system. It ferries oxygen and food to your cells. It washes away waste to your liver and kidneys for disposal, and it rushes in special cells to fight off infection. It even keeps you warm! No wonder it's such a complex stew!

BLOOD PLASMA

All of the ingredients float in a yellowish fluid called plasma. Plasma makes up just over half your blood and it is mostly water.

RED BLOOD CELLS

Your blood is red because it is jam-packed with 25 trillion button-shaped red cells, and the body makes 2 million new ones every second. They are constantly in action carrying oxygen swiftly from your lungs to your body.

YOUR OWN BLOOD

If you lose too much blood, you may be saved by a transfusion from someone else. For this to work, the new blood must be the right type. There are four main groups of human blood (called O, A, B and AB), and they don't mix, because your body's immune system will fight against blood from the wrong group.

1. LOADING UP

Red blood cells contain special tangly molecules called hemoglobin. When the blood cells sweep past your lungs, hemoglobin grabs a load of oxygen.

2. GLOWING

Hemoglobin glows red when it has a load of oxygen, turning your blood bright red. Blood cells carrying oxygen are pumped to where they're needed.

3. LETTING GO

When a red blood cell reaches its destination, the hemoglobin lets the oxygen go. The cell stops glowing and turns purple. It's now ready to pick up another load.

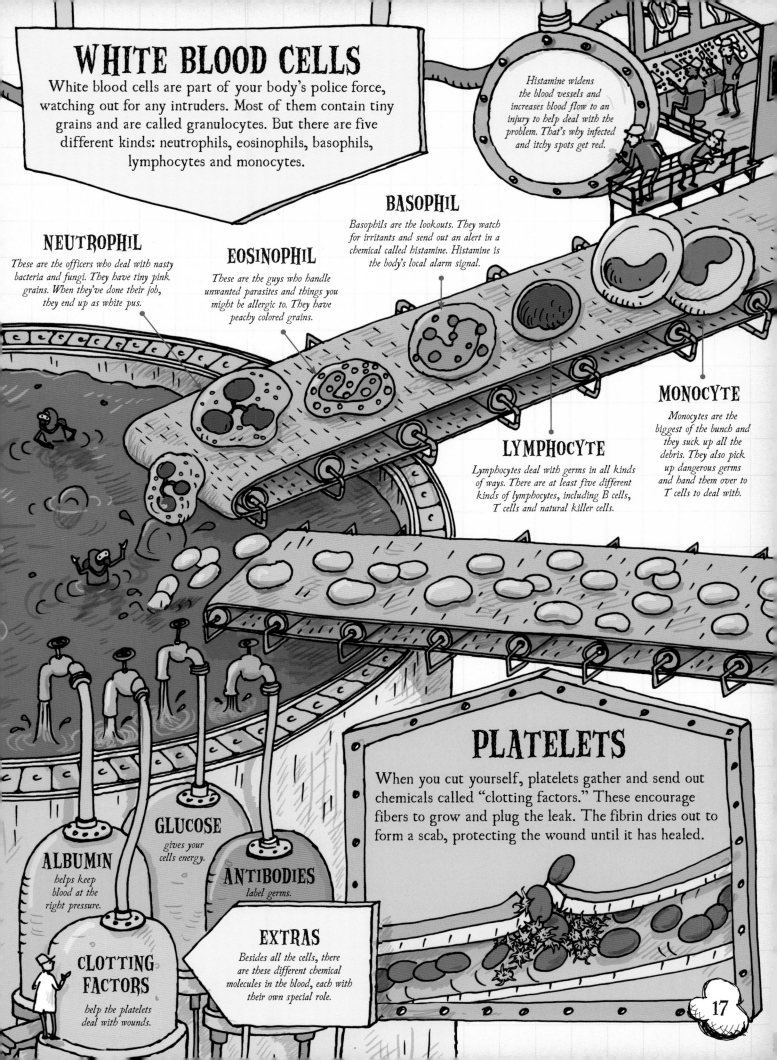

WHITE BLOOD CELLS

White blood cells are part of your body's police force, watching out for any intruders. Most of them contain tiny grains and are called granulocytes. But there are five different kinds: neutrophils, eosinophils, basophils, lymphocytes and monocytes.

Histamine widens the blood vessels and increases blood flow to an injury to help deal with the problem. That's why infected and itchy spots get red.

BASOPHIL

Basophils are the lookouts. They watch for irritants and send out an alert in a chemical called histamine. Histamine is the body's local alarm signal.

NEUTROPHIL

These are the officers who deal with nasty bacteria and fungi. They have tiny pink grains. When they've done their job, they end up as white pus.

EOSINOPHIL

These are the guys who handle unwanted parasites and things you might be allergic to. They have peachy colored grains.

MONOCYTE

Monocytes are the biggest of the bunch and they suck up all the debris. They also pick up dangerous germs and hand them over to T cells to deal with.

LYMPHOCYTE

Lymphocytes deal with germs in all kinds of ways. There are at least five different kinds of lymphocytes, including B cells, T cells and natural killer cells.

ALBUMIN
helps keep blood at the right pressure.

GLUCOSE
gives your cells energy.

ANTIBODIES
label germs.

CLOTTING FACTORS
help the platelets deal with wounds.

EXTRAS
Besides all the cells, there are these different chemical molecules in the blood, each with their own special role.

PLATELETS

When you cut yourself, platelets gather and send out chemicals called "clotting factors." These encourage fibers to grow and plug the leak. The fibrin dries out to form a scab, protecting the wound until it has healed.

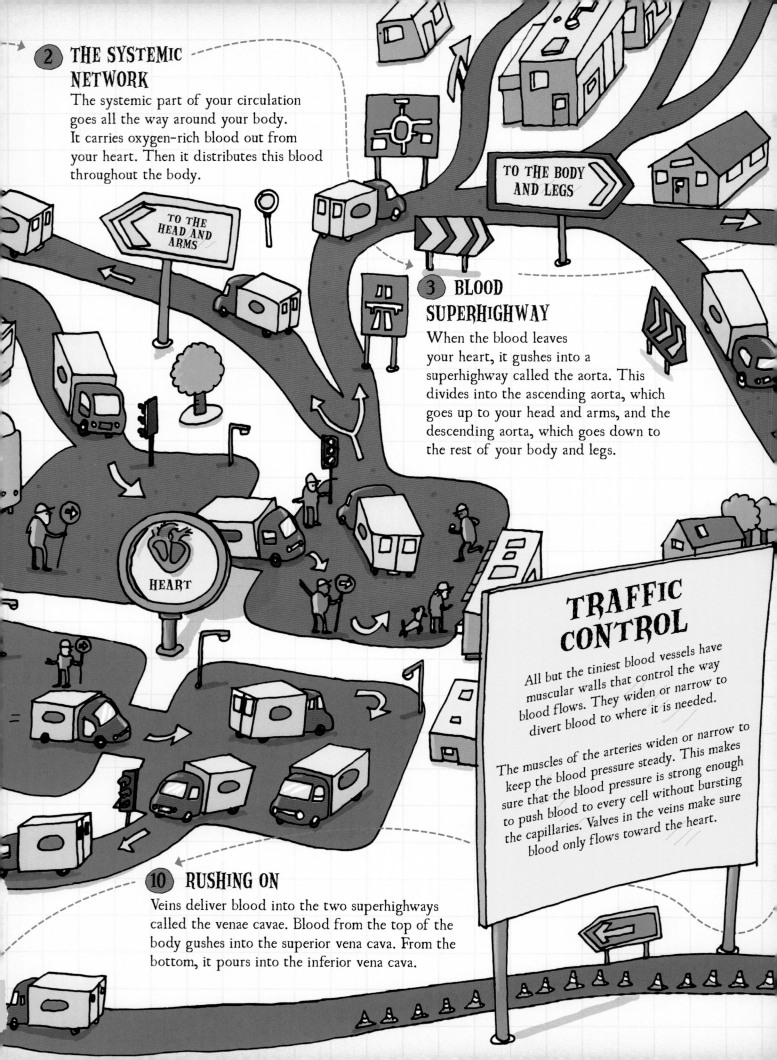

2 THE SYSTEMIC NETWORK

The systemic part of your circulation goes all the way around your body. It carries oxygen-rich blood out from your heart. Then it distributes this blood throughout the body.

TO THE HEAD AND ARMS

TO THE BODY AND LEGS

3 BLOOD SUPERHIGHWAY

When the blood leaves your heart, it gushes into a superhighway called the aorta. This divides into the ascending aorta, which goes up to your head and arms, and the descending aorta, which goes down to the rest of your body and legs.

HEART

TRAFFIC CONTROL

All but the tiniest blood vessels have muscular walls that control the way blood flows. They widen or narrow to divert blood to where it is needed.

The muscles of the arteries widen or narrow to keep the blood pressure steady. This makes sure that the blood pressure is strong enough to push blood to every cell without bursting the capillaries. Valves in the veins make sure blood only flows toward the heart.

10 RUSHING ON

Veins deliver blood into the two superhighways called the venae cavae. Blood from the top of the body gushes into the superior vena cava. From the bottom, it pours into the inferior vena cava.

WHERE DOES BLOOD GO?

Your body cells need a nonstop supply of oxygen and it's your blood's task to give it to them. Pumped by your heart, blood picks up oxygen from your lungs and distributes it through a network of pipes. It then travels back again to your lungs to collect more oxygen.

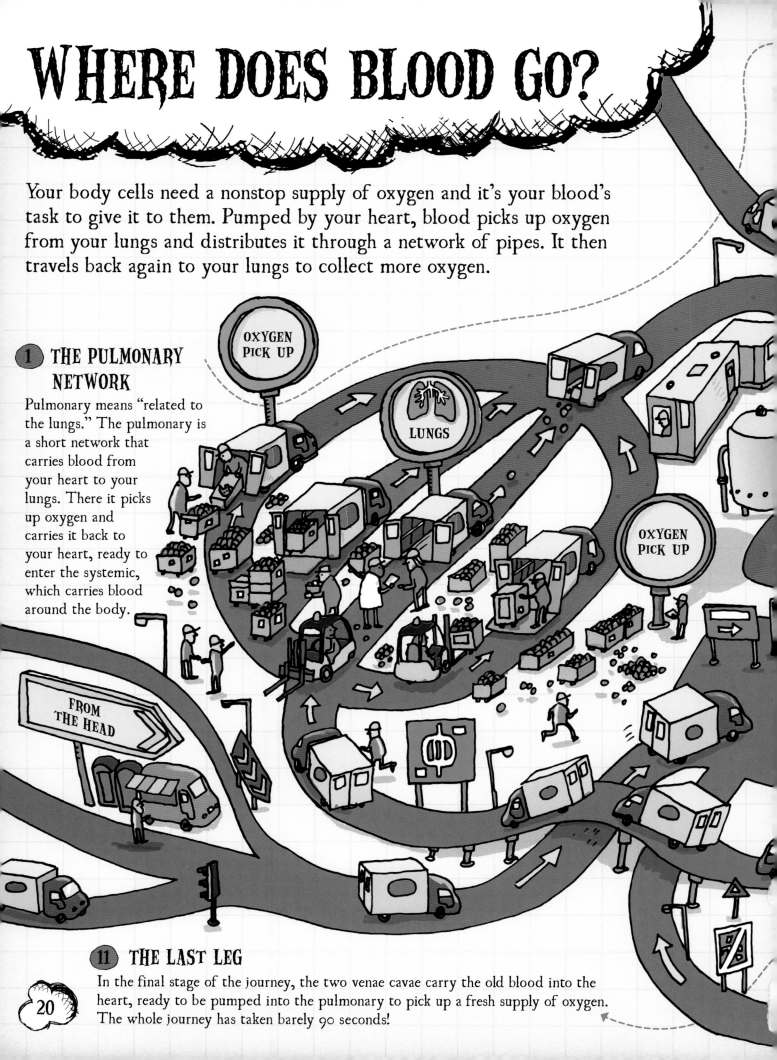

1 THE PULMONARY NETWORK

Pulmonary means "related to the lungs." The pulmonary is a short network that carries blood from your heart to your lungs. There it picks up oxygen and carries it back to your heart, ready to enter the systemic, which carries blood around the body.

OXYGEN PICK UP

LUNGS

OXYGEN PICK UP

FROM THE HEAD

11 THE LAST LEG

In the final stage of the journey, the two venae cavae carry the old blood into the heart, ready to be pumped into the pulmonary to pick up a fresh supply of oxygen. The whole journey has taken barely 90 seconds!

20

HOW DOES YOUR HEART BEAT?

Your heart is a tiny super-pump. Every moment of your life, it is busy squeezing away, driving blood around your body. It can do this because it's made of special "cardiac" muscle that contracts and relaxes automatically.

1 GET READY...

Every time your heart beats, it goes through the same sequence, called the cardiac cycle, as each chamber contracts (systole phase) and relaxes (diastole phase). It all begins with the heart muscles relaxed, and blood slowly filling up each atria.

DOUBLE PUMP

Your heart is not one pump but two, separated by a thick wall down the middle called the septum. The left side is the stronger pump because it pumps blood laden with oxygen from the lungs all around your body. The right side is weaker as it only has to pump blood through the lungs to pick up oxygen.

2 SQUEEZE!

A wave of contraction sweeps down from the top of the heart from left to right, squeezing each atrium in systole. As each atrium is squeezed, the blood in it pushes against the valve into the ventricle. The valve swings open like a trapdoor and blood floods through.

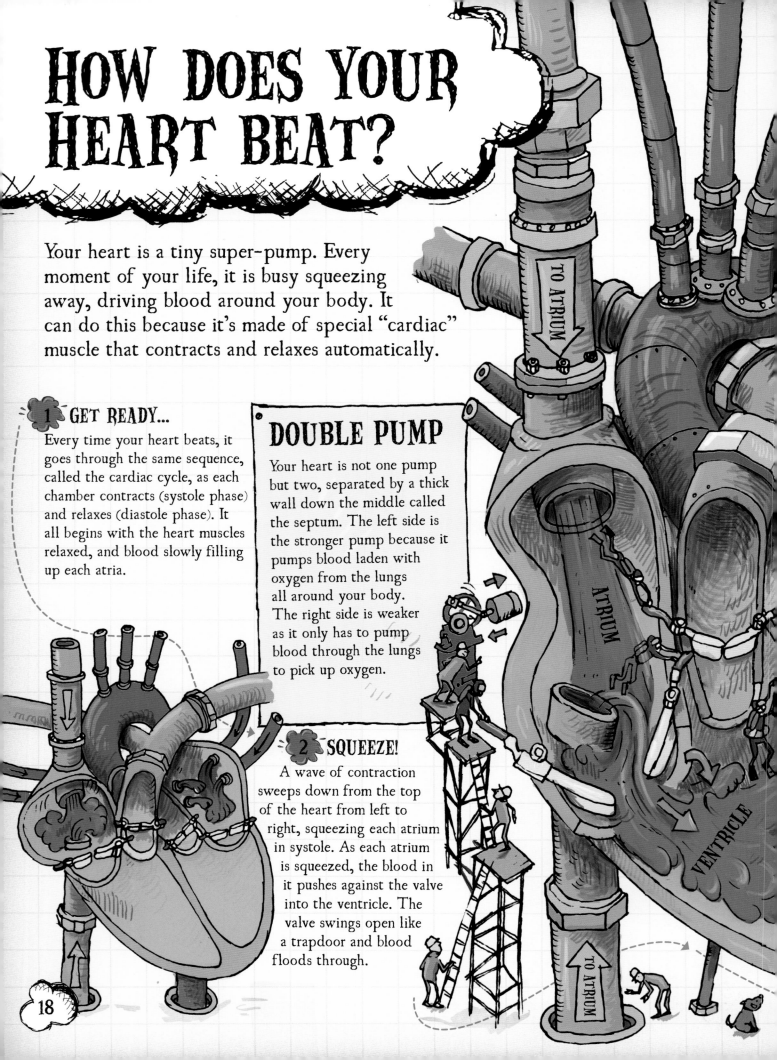

TO ATRIUM

ATRIUM

VENTRICLE

TO ATRIUM

HOW DO YOU MOVE?

You need muscles to move and even to sit still. Without muscles, you'd slump like an old coat. Muscles are amazing little motors that work whenever you want them to, instantly, by tensing and relaxing.

INVOLUNTARY MUSCLES

Muscles inside you work pretty much automatically, making things move without you ever thinking about it, even when you're fast asleep.

There are two kinds of involuntary muscle: smooth and cardiac. Smooth muscles, as in your gut and blood vessels, are made in sheets that form tubes or bags. The other type of involuntary muscle is cardiac muscle, which powers your heart.

MUSCLES ON DEMAND

You have two kinds of muscle. There are more than 650 "voluntary" or "skeletal" muscles covering your skeleton that you can control with your thoughts. These are the muscles you move with. There are also "involuntary" muscles inside you which automatically control body functions such as your heartbeat.

MARATHON MUSCLE

Cardiac muscle is the special muscle that makes your heart beat. Its combination of striped muscle (see below) and smooth muscle is built for endurance. It contracts at least once a second every moment of your life.

MUSCLE FOR BREATHING

Your diaphragm is a sheet of muscle that stretches across the inside of your midriff and helps you breathe. Unusual for an inside muscle, it is skeletal muscle. Most of the time it works automatically, but you can control it by thinking.

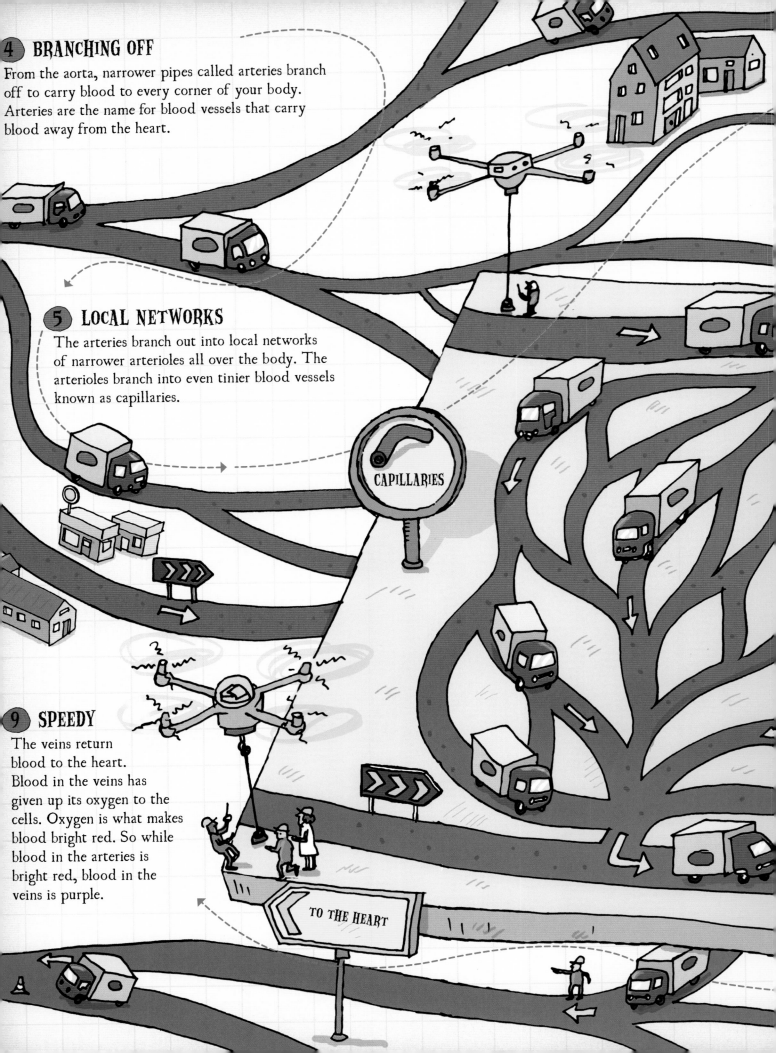

4 BRANCHING OFF

From the aorta, narrower pipes called arteries branch off to carry blood to every corner of your body. Arteries are the name for blood vessels that carry blood away from the heart.

5 LOCAL NETWORKS

The arteries branch out into local networks of narrower arterioles all over the body. The arterioles branch into even tinier blood vessels known as capillaries.

CAPILLARIES

9 SPEEDY

The veins return blood to the heart. Blood in the veins has given up its oxygen to the cells. Oxygen is what makes blood bright red. So while blood in the arteries is bright red, blood in the veins is purple.

TO THE HEART

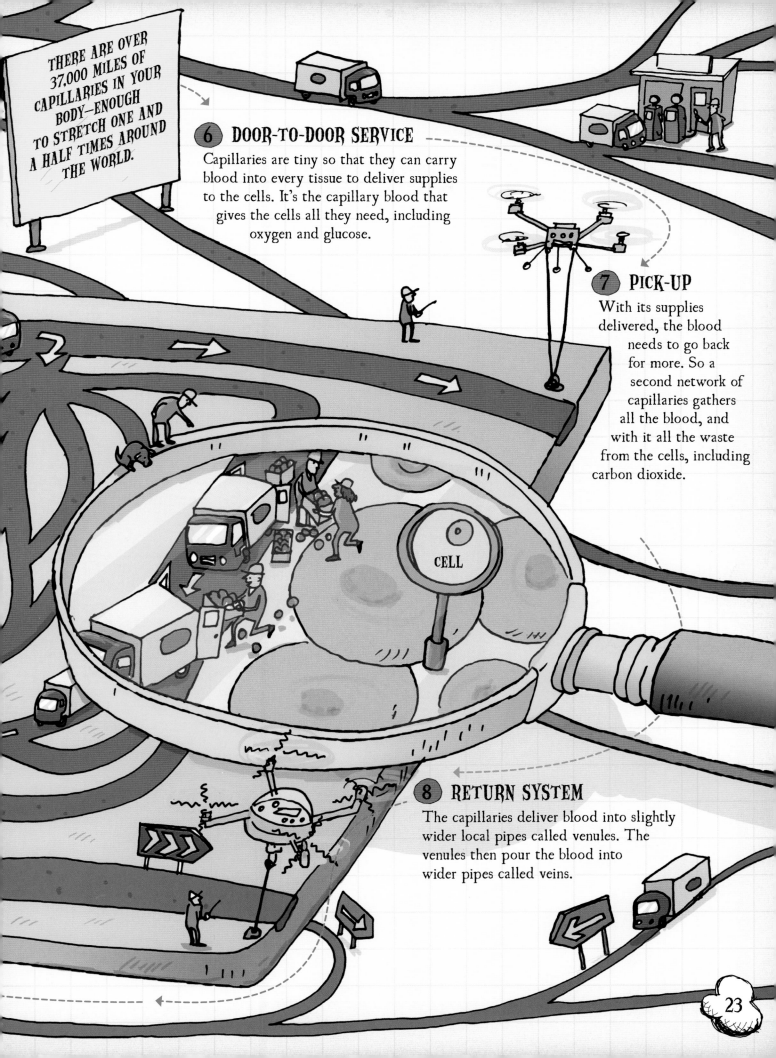

THERE ARE OVER 37,000 MILES OF CAPILLARIES IN YOUR BODY—ENOUGH TO STRETCH ONE AND A HALF TIMES AROUND THE WORLD.

6 DOOR-TO-DOOR SERVICE

Capillaries are tiny so that they can carry blood into every tissue to deliver supplies to the cells. It's the capillary blood that gives the cells all they need, including oxygen and glucose.

7 PICK-UP

With its supplies delivered, the blood needs to go back for more. So a second network of capillaries gathers all the blood, and with it all the waste from the cells, including carbon dioxide.

CELL

8 RETURN SYSTEM

The capillaries deliver blood into slightly wider local pipes called venules. The venules then pour the blood into wider pipes called veins.

DOUBLE CHAMBER

Each side of your heart has two chambers. There is an atrium at the top, where blood builds up, and a ventricle at the bottom, which is the main pumping chamber. Each atrium and ventricle is separated by a large valve. Each ventricle also has a smaller valve to let blood out.

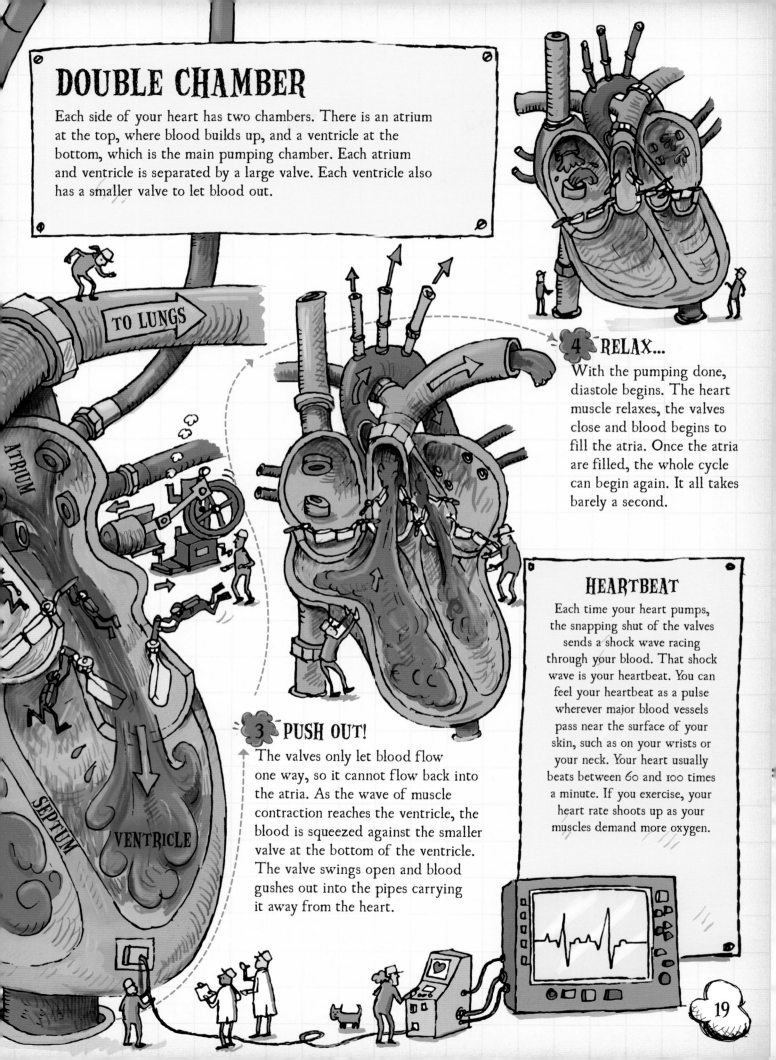

TO LUNGS

ATRIUM

SEPTUM

VENTRICLE

4 RELAX...

With the pumping done, diastole begins. The heart muscle relaxes, the valves close and blood begins to fill the atria. Once the atria are filled, the whole cycle can begin again. It all takes barely a second.

3 PUSH OUT!

The valves only let blood flow one way, so it cannot flow back into the atria. As the wave of muscle contraction reaches the ventricle, the blood is squeezed against the smaller valve at the bottom of the ventricle. The valve swings open and blood gushes out into the pipes carrying it away from the heart.

HEARTBEAT

Each time your heart pumps, the snapping shut of the valves sends a shock wave racing through your blood. That shock wave is your heartbeat. You can feel your heartbeat as a pulse wherever major blood vessels pass near the surface of your skin, such as on your wrists or your neck. Your heart usually beats between 60 and 100 times a minute. If you exercise, your heart rate shoots up as your muscles demand more oxygen.

19

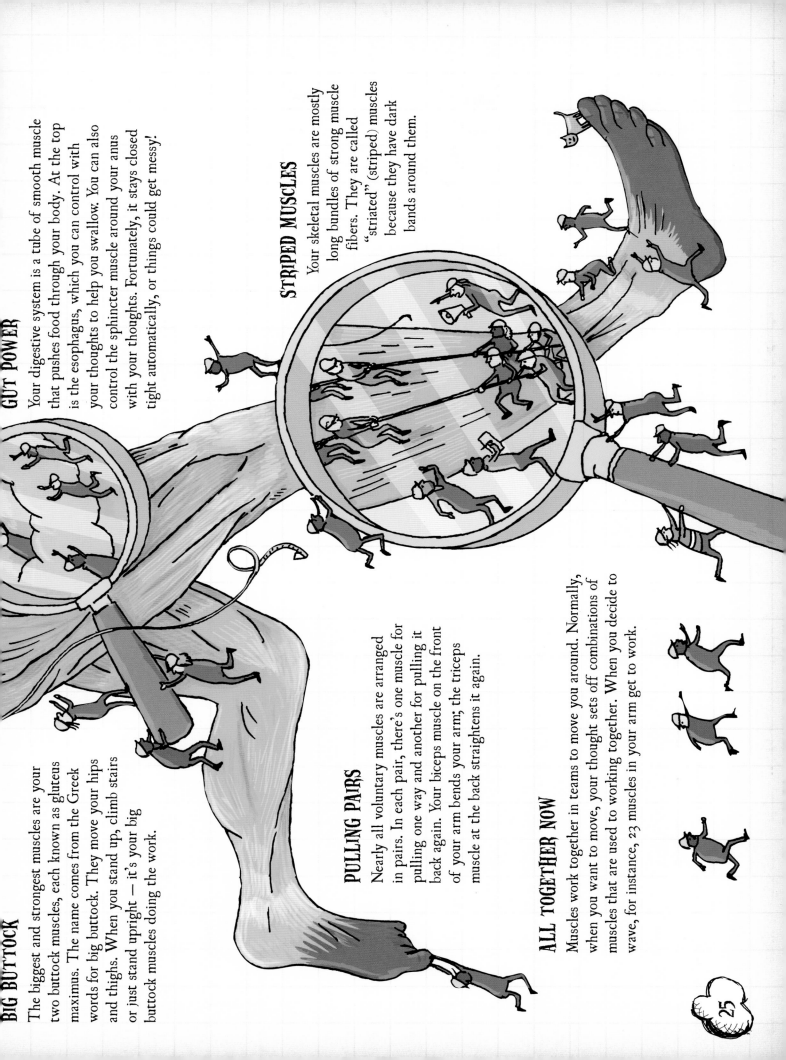

BIG BUTTOCK

The biggest and strongest muscles are your two buttock muscles, each known as gluteus maximus. The name comes from the Greek words for big buttock. They move your hips and thighs. When you stand up, climb stairs or just stand upright — it's your big buttock muscles doing the work.

GUT POWER

Your digestive system is a tube of smooth muscle that pushes food through your body. At the top is the esophagus, which you can control with your thoughts to help you swallow. You can also control the sphincter muscle around your anus with your thoughts. Fortunately, it stays closed tight automatically, or things could get messy!

STRIPED MUSCLES

Your skeletal muscles are mostly long bundles of strong muscle fibers. They are called "striated" (striped) muscles because they have dark bands around them.

PULLING PAIRS

Nearly all voluntary muscles are arranged in pairs. In each pair, there's one muscle for pulling one way and another for pulling it back again. Your biceps muscle on the front of your arm bends your arm; the triceps muscle at the back straightens it again.

ALL TOGETHER NOW

Muscles work together in teams to move you around. Normally, when you want to move, your thought sets off combinations of muscles that are used to working together. When you decide to wave, for instance, 23 muscles in your arm get to work.

HOW DO MUSCLES WORK?

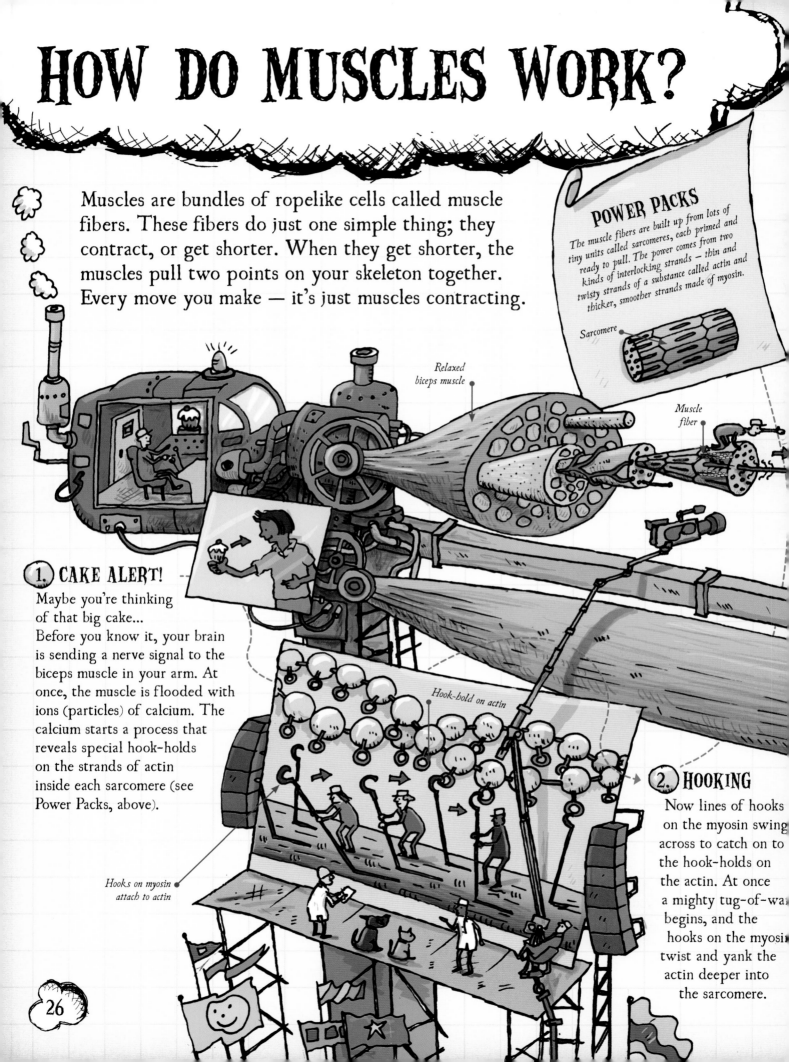

Muscles are bundles of ropelike cells called muscle fibers. These fibers do just one simple thing; they contract, or get shorter. When they get shorter, the muscles pull two points on your skeleton together. Every move you make — it's just muscles contracting.

POWER PACKS

The muscle fibers are built up from lots of tiny units called sarcomeres, each primed and ready to pull. The power comes from two kinds of interlocking strands — thin and twisty strands of a substance called actin and thicker, smoother strands made of myosin.

Sarcomere

Relaxed biceps muscle

Muscle fiber

1. CAKE ALERT!

Maybe you're thinking of that big cake...
Before you know it, your brain is sending a nerve signal to the biceps muscle in your arm. At once, the muscle is flooded with ions (particles) of calcium. The calcium starts a process that reveals special hook-holds on the strands of actin inside each sarcomere (see Power Packs, above).

Hook-hold on actin

Hooks on myosin attach to actin

2. HOOKING

Now lines of hooks on the myosin swing across to catch on to the hook-holds on the actin. At once a mighty tug-of-war begins, and the hooks on the myosin twist and yank the actin deeper into the sarcomere.

26

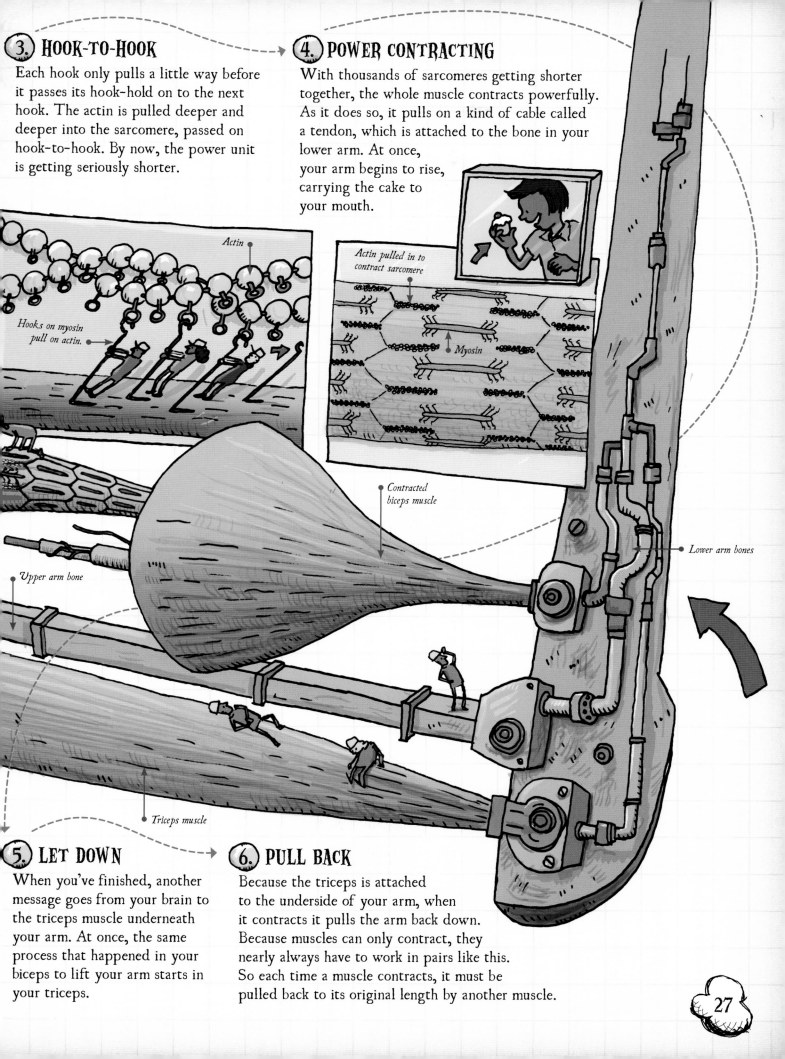

3. HOOK-TO-HOOK

Each hook only pulls a little way before it passes its hook-hold on to the next hook. The actin is pulled deeper and deeper into the sarcomere, passed on hook-to-hook. By now, the power unit is getting seriously shorter.

4. POWER CONTRACTING

With thousands of sarcomeres getting shorter together, the whole muscle contracts powerfully. As it does so, it pulls on a kind of cable called a tendon, which is attached to the bone in your lower arm. At once, your arm begins to rise, carrying the cake to your mouth.

Actin

Hooks on myosin pull on actin.

Actin pulled in to contract sarcomere

Myosin

Contracted biceps muscle

Upper arm bone

Lower arm bones

Triceps muscle

5. LET DOWN

When you've finished, another message goes from your brain to the triceps muscle underneath your arm. At once, the same process that happened in your biceps to lift your arm starts in your triceps.

6. PULL BACK

Because the triceps is attached to the underside of your arm, when it contracts it pulls the arm back down. Because muscles can only contract, they nearly always have to work in pairs like this. So each time a muscle contracts, it must be pulled back to its original length by another muscle.

HOW DO YOU GET STRONG?

Many people go through life without doing much exercise at all. But top athletes train hard to get super-fit and strong. They have to work hard with exercises, such as running and gym routines.

OXYGEN

1. MUSCLE FUEL

Your muscles need fuel, just like a car engine, and their fuel is glucose, supplied in the blood. They get their energy when glucose combines with oxygen in a process called aerobic respiration.

GLUCOSE

HEART MONITOR

♥

GLUCOSE   OXYGEN

LACTIC ACID LEVEL

LOW   HIGH

2. WORKING HARD

When you exercise hard, your muscles may work so hard that your blood supply can't keep up. When this happens, your muscles burn glucose without oxygen. This is anaerobic respiration.

3. ACID BUILD-UP

If you're unfit, your muscles go on working anaerobically much longer. This not only uses up glucose faster and tires you out, it also lets lactic acid build up in your muscles so they feel sore. When you finally stop running, you may have to pant to get extra oxygen to burn off the acid.

4. WORKING AEROBICALLY

If you're fit, your heart starts pumping harder and boosts the blood supply to deliver more oxygen and switch the muscles to aerobic respiration. In a long race, an athlete's muscles will work aerobically for most of the time — and only switch to anaerobic for the final sprint.

5. GROWING MUSCLES

When you exercise, your muscles grow larger. At first, the fibers just get fatter. But if you go on exercising regularly, you actually grow new muscle fibers, which means they grow stronger. The blood supply also improves, so they can work for longer.

6. STRONG HEART

Regular exercise improves fitness by bulking up your muscles, strengthening your heart, and building up your body's ability to pump blood and supply muscles with oxygen. But for it to work like this, exercise has to be aerobic.

DON'T PUSH IT

During exercise, your body diverts blood to the skeletal muscles so they get more oxygen. Usually, this has little effect on the rest of the body. But if you exercise hard, the supply to your heart can drop. That's why unfit runners can suffer heart attacks.

OXYGEN LEVEL

HOW DO YOU SPEAK?

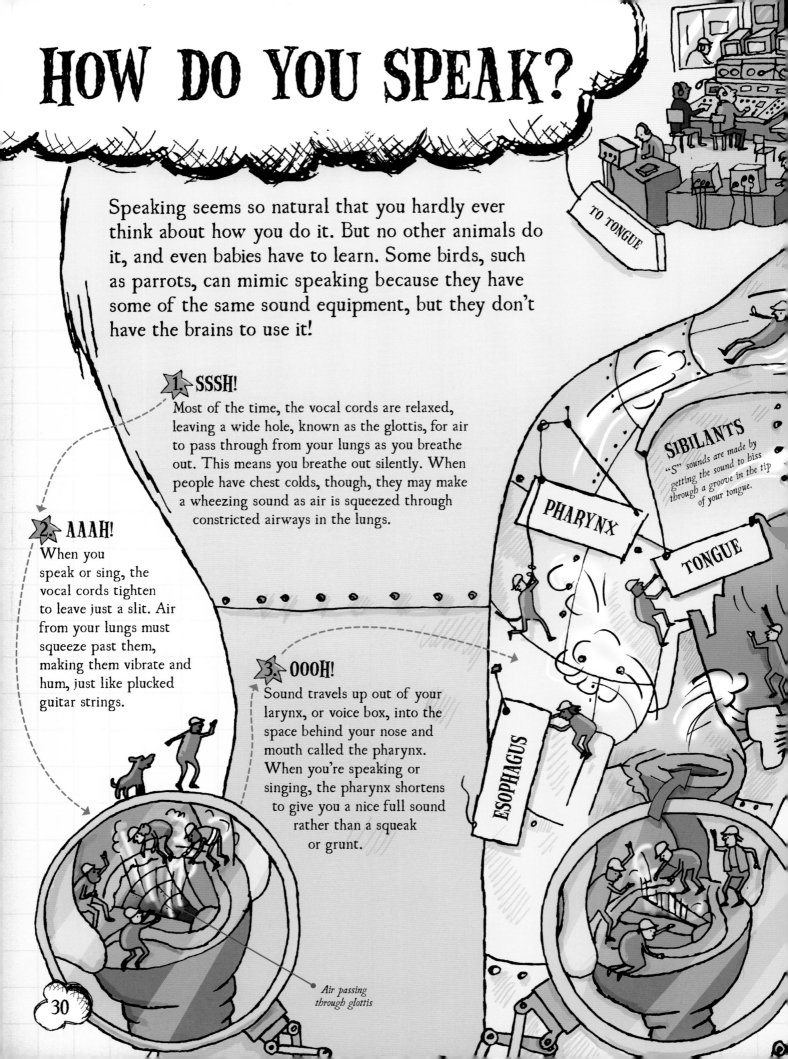

Speaking seems so natural that you hardly ever think about how you do it. But no other animals do it, and even babies have to learn. Some birds, such as parrots, can mimic speaking because they have some of the same sound equipment, but they don't have the brains to use it!

TO TONGUE

1. SSSH!

Most of the time, the vocal cords are relaxed, leaving a wide hole, known as the glottis, for air to pass through from your lungs as you breathe out. This means you breathe out silently. When people have chest colds, though, they may make a wheezing sound as air is squeezed through constricted airways in the lungs.

2. AAAH!

When you speak or sing, the vocal cords tighten to leave just a slit. Air from your lungs must squeeze past them, making them vibrate and hum, just like plucked guitar strings.

3. OOOH!

Sound travels up out of your larynx, or voice box, into the space behind your nose and mouth called the pharynx. When you're speaking or singing, the pharynx shortens to give you a nice full sound rather than a squeak or grunt.

SIBILANTS
"S" sounds are made by getting the sound to hiss through a groove in the tip of your tongue.

PHARYNX

TONGUE

ESOPHAGUS

Air passing through glottis

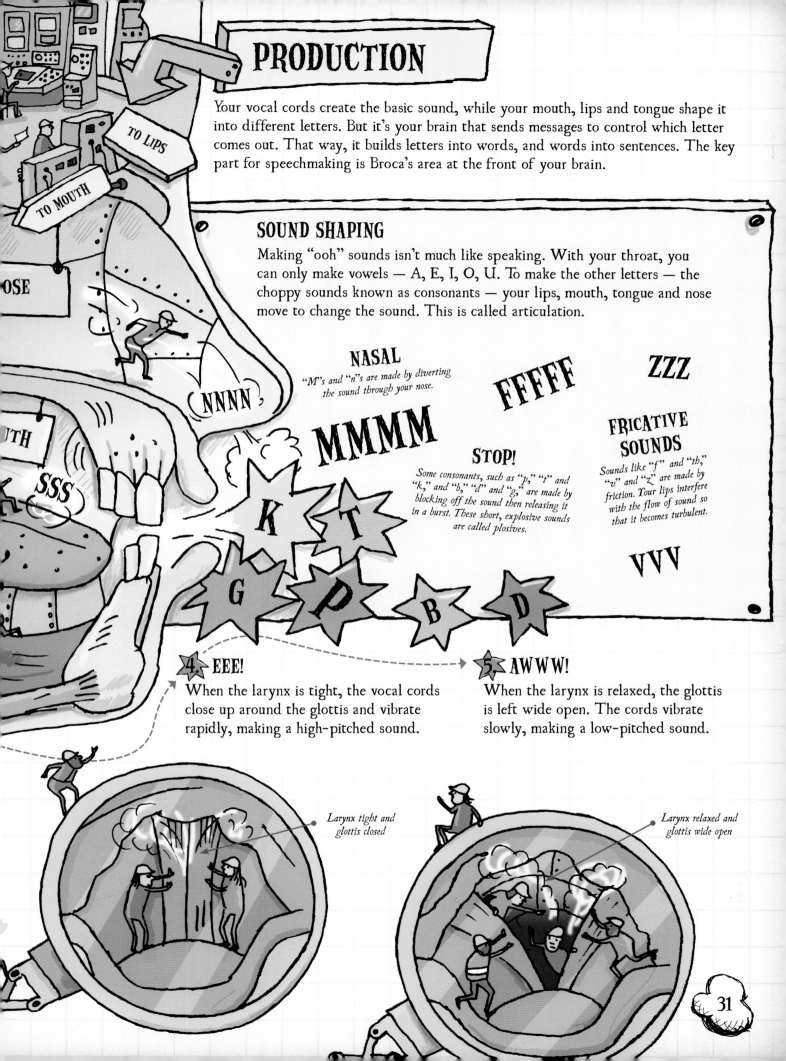

PRODUCTION

Your vocal cords create the basic sound, while your mouth, lips and tongue shape it into different letters. But it's your brain that sends messages to control which letter comes out. That way, it builds letters into words, and words into sentences. The key part for speechmaking is Broca's area at the front of your brain.

TO LIPS

TO MOUTH

OSE

UTH

SSS

SOUND SHAPING

Making "ooh" sounds isn't much like speaking. With your throat, you can only make vowels — A, E, I, O, U. To make the other letters — the choppy sounds known as consonants — your lips, mouth, tongue and nose move to change the sound. This is called articulation.

NASAL
"M's and "n"s are made by diverting the sound through your nose.

NNNN

MMMM

FFFFF

STOP!
Some consonants, such as "p," "t" and "k," and "b," "d" and "g," are made by blocking off the sound then releasing it in a burst. These short, explosive sounds are called plosives.

ZZZ

FRICATIVE SOUNDS
Sounds like "f" and "th," "v" and "z" are made by friction. Your lips interfere with the flow of sound so that it becomes turbulent.

VVV

K T G P B D

4. EEE!
When the larynx is tight, the vocal cords close up around the glottis and vibrate rapidly, making a high-pitched sound.

5. AWWW!
When the larynx is relaxed, the glottis is left wide open. The cords vibrate slowly, making a low-pitched sound.

Larynx tight and glottis closed

Larynx relaxed and glottis wide open

WHAT'S ON YOUR OUTSIDE?

Your skin is your body's outer casing and the biggest organ in the body. It's pretty much waterproof and germproof. It insulates your body from the cold and lets out excess heat. It tells you about the world by responding to touch. It even gives you nourishment by making vitamin D from sunlight. It is less than one tenth of an inch thick, but it's made of many layers.

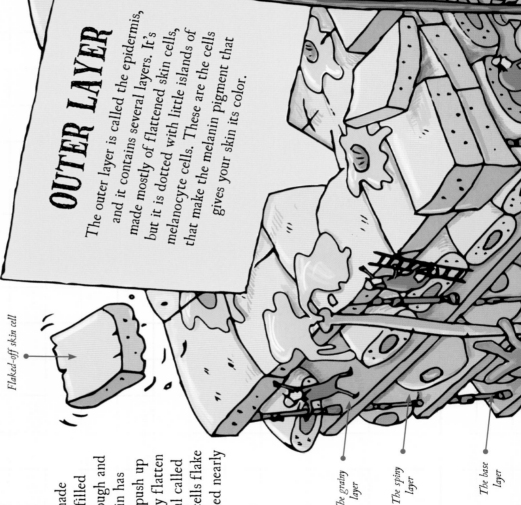

Outer layer of the epidermis

OUTER LAYER

The outer layer is called the epidermis, and it contains several layers. It's made mostly of flattened skin cells, but it is dotted with little islands of melanocyte cells. These are the cells that make the melanin pigment that gives your skin its color.

Flaked-off skin cell

The grainy layer

The spiny layer

The base layer

1. LOSING YOUR SKIN

The outer layer of the epidermis is made mostly from dead and dying keratin-filled cells. These leathery cells are both tough and disposable. To stay effective, your skin has to be constantly renewed. New cells push up all the time to the surface, where they flatten and die and turn into a tough material called keratin. Over 40,000 of these dead cells flake off every minute. In your life, you shed nearly 110 pounds of skin!

2. TOUGHENING UP: THE GRAINY LAYER

In the grainy layer, skin cells lose their nuclei and look grainy. The cells start to die and fill up with tough keratin fibers. This process is called cornification.

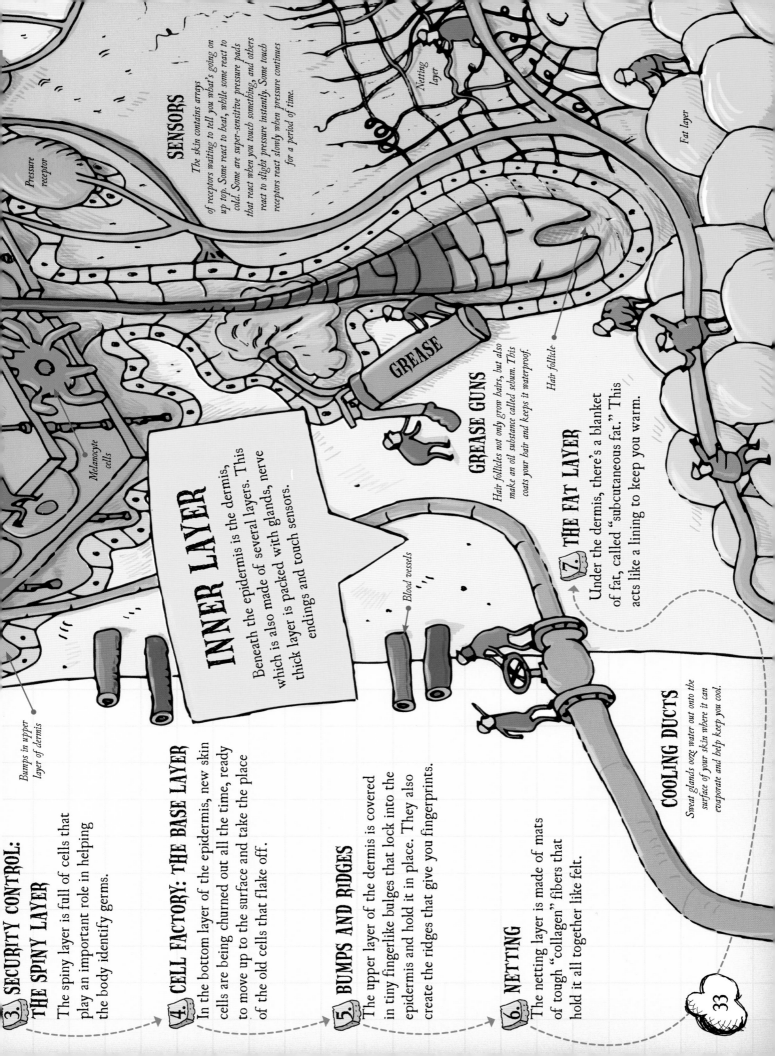

SENSORS

The skin contains arrays of receptors waiting to tell you what's going on up top. Some react to heat, while some react to cold. Some are super-sensitive pressure pads that react when you touch something, and others react to slight pressure instantly. Some touch receptors react slowly when pressure continues for a period of time.

Pressure receptor

Netting layer

Fat layer

GREASE

Melanocyte cells

Hair follicle

INNER LAYER

Beneath the epidermis is the dermis. This is also made of several layers. This thick layer is packed with glands, nerve endings and touch sensors.

GREASE GUNS

Hair follicles not only grow hairs, but also make an oil substance called sebum. This coats your hair and keeps it waterproof.

Blood vessels

7. THE FAT LAYER

Under the dermis, there's a blanket of fat, called "subcutaneous fat." This acts like a lining to keep you warm.

Bumps in upper layer of dermis

3. SECURITY CONTROL: THE SPINY LAYER

The spiny layer is full of cells that play an important role in helping the body identify germs.

4. CELL FACTORY: THE BASE LAYER

In the bottom layer of the epidermis, new skin cells are being churned out all the time, ready to move up to the surface and take the place of the old cells that flake off.

5. BUMPS AND RIDGES

The upper layer of the dermis is covered in tiny fingerlike bulges that lock into the epidermis and hold it in place. They also create the ridges that give you fingerprints.

6. NETTING

The netting layer is made of mats of tough "collagen" fibers that hold it all together like felt.

COOLING DUCTS

Sweat glands ooze water out onto the surface of your skin where it can evaporate and help keep you cool.

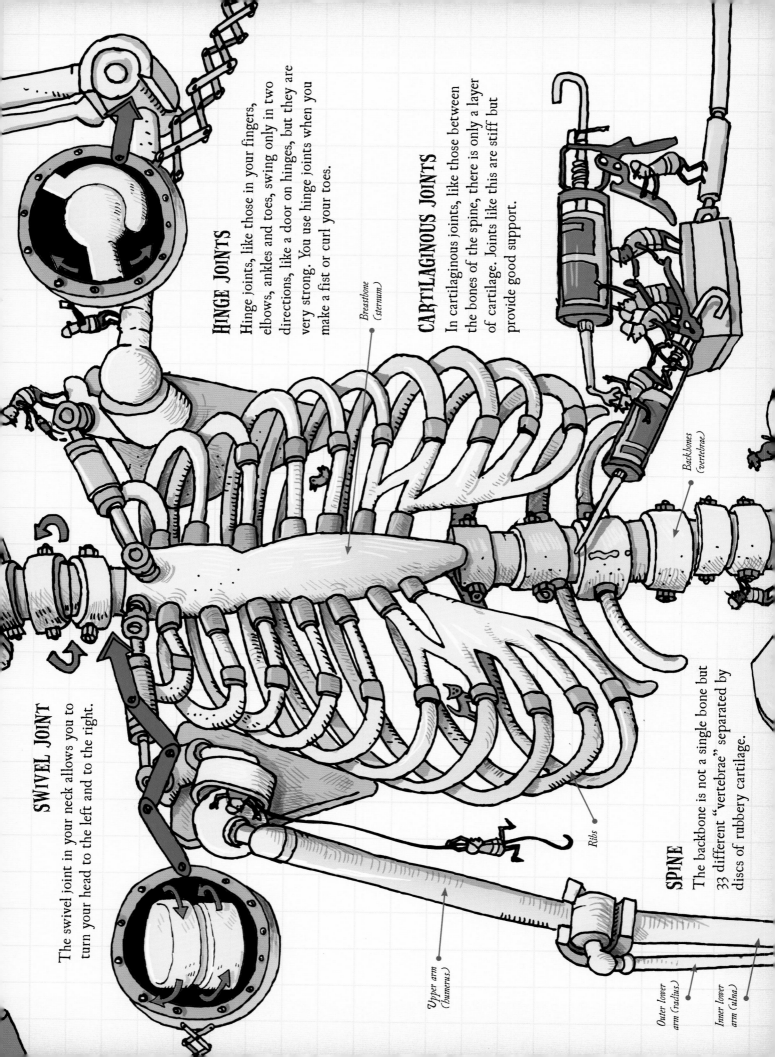

SWIVEL JOINT

The swivel joint in your neck allows you to turn your head to the left and to the right.

HINGE JOINTS

Hinge joints, like those in your fingers, elbows, ankles and toes, swing only in two directions, like a door on hinges, but they are very strong. You use hinge joints when you make a fist or curl your toes.

Breastbone (sternum)

CARTILAGINOUS JOINTS

In cartilaginous joints, like those between the bones of the spine, there is only a layer of cartilage. Joints like this are stiff but provide good support.

Backbones (vertebrae)

Ribs

SPINE

The backbone is not a single bone but 33 different "vertebrae" separated by discs of rubbery cartilage.

Upper arm (humerus)

Outer lower arm (radius)

Inner lower arm (ulna)

WHAT'S HOLDING YOU TOGETHER?

Your skeleton is the framework of bones that holds your body together. It provides anchor points for the muscles you use to move. It supports your skin and other tissues, and protects your heart, brain and other organs. You have more than 200 bones, cushioned by rubbery cartilage and tied together with fibers called ligaments.

AXIAL SKELETON

Your axial skeleton is the core of your skeleton at the top. It's made of your skull, spine and ribcage. It contains more than 80 bones in adults.

APPENDICULAR SKELETON

Your appendicular skeleton is the rest of your skeleton, built out from the axial skeleton — your shoulders, arms and hands, hips, legs and feet. It's made of over 120 bones.

JOINTS

Even though your skeleton is strong and rigid, it can bend and move in almost any direction. That's because it is made of separate bones held together at joints. Joints are where bones meet. All your bones except one (the hyoid bone in your neck) form a joint with another bone. Joints allow nearly all your bones to move independently.

FIBROUS JOINTS

The joints in your skull are bound so tightly together by fibers that they are fixed firmly in place and cannot move.

SADDLE JOINTS

The joints in your thumb are saddle-joints. In these, two saddle-shaped bones fit snugly together and can rock to and fro and from side to side. They are strong but can't rotate much.

Skull (cranium)

Lower jaw (mandible)

WHAT ARE BONES?

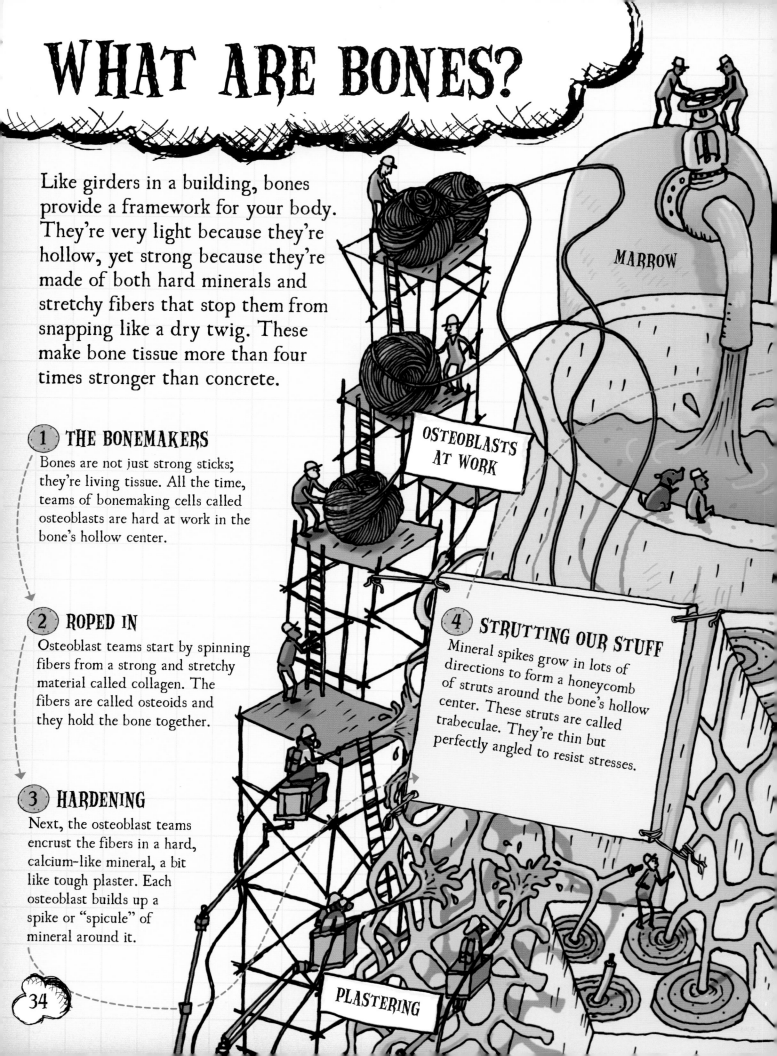

Like girders in a building, bones provide a framework for your body. They're very light because they're hollow, yet strong because they're made of both hard minerals and stretchy fibers that stop them from snapping like a dry twig. These make bone tissue more than four times stronger than concrete.

1 THE BONEMAKERS

Bones are not just strong sticks; they're living tissue. All the time, teams of bonemaking cells called osteoblasts are hard at work in the bone's hollow center.

2 ROPED IN

Osteoblast teams start by spinning fibers from a strong and stretchy material called collagen. The fibers are called osteoids and they hold the bone together.

3 HARDENING

Next, the osteoblast teams encrust the fibers in a hard, calcium-like mineral, a bit like tough plaster. Each osteoblast builds up a spike or "spicule" of mineral around it.

MARROW

OSTEOBLASTS AT WORK

4 STRUTTING OUR STUFF

Mineral spikes grow in lots of directions to form a honeycomb of struts around the bone's hollow center. These struts are called trabeculae. They're thin but perfectly angled to resist stresses.

PLASTERING

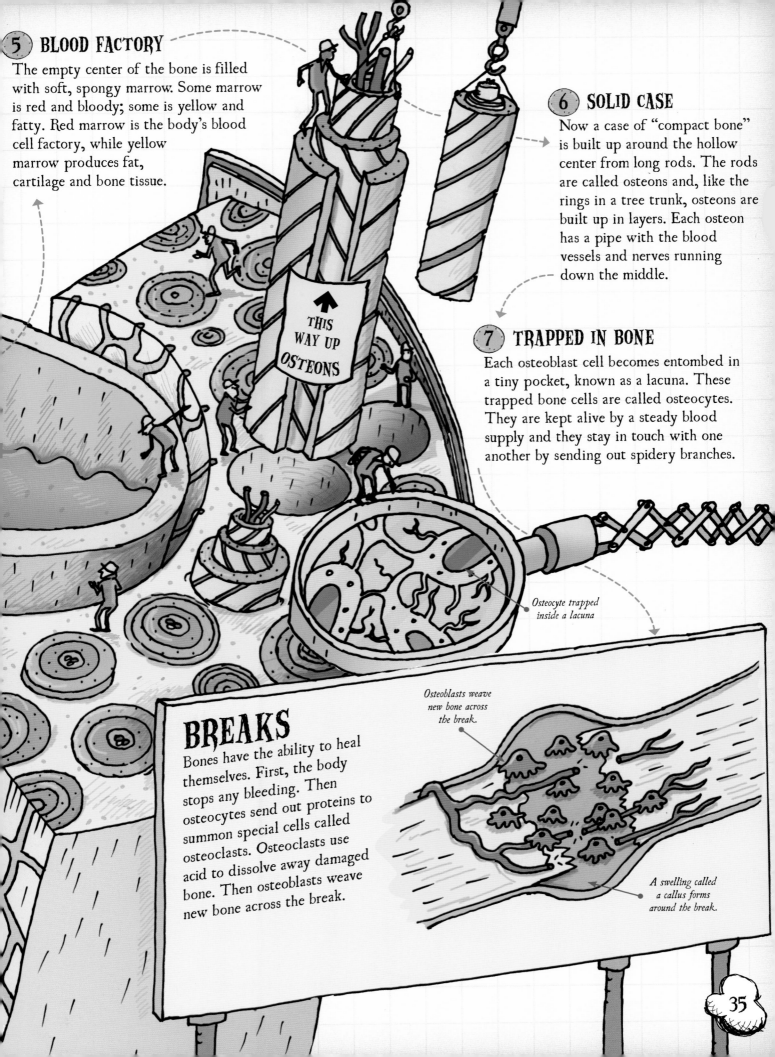

5 BLOOD FACTORY

The empty center of the bone is filled with soft, spongy marrow. Some marrow is red and bloody; some is yellow and fatty. Red marrow is the body's blood cell factory, while yellow marrow produces fat, cartilage and bone tissue.

THIS WAY UP OSTEONS

6 SOLID CASE

Now a case of "compact bone" is built up around the hollow center from long rods. The rods are called osteons and, like the rings in a tree trunk, osteons are built up in layers. Each osteon has a pipe with the blood vessels and nerves running down the middle.

7 TRAPPED IN BONE

Each osteoblast cell becomes entombed in a tiny pocket, known as a lacuna. These trapped bone cells are called osteocytes. They are kept alive by a steady blood supply and they stay in touch with one another by sending out spidery branches.

Osteocyte trapped inside a lacuna

BREAKS

Bones have the ability to heal themselves. First, the body stops any bleeding. Then osteocytes send out proteins to summon special cells called osteoclasts. Osteoclasts use acid to dissolve away damaged bone. Then osteoblasts weave new bone across the break.

Osteoblasts weave new bone across the break.

A swelling called a callus forms around the break.

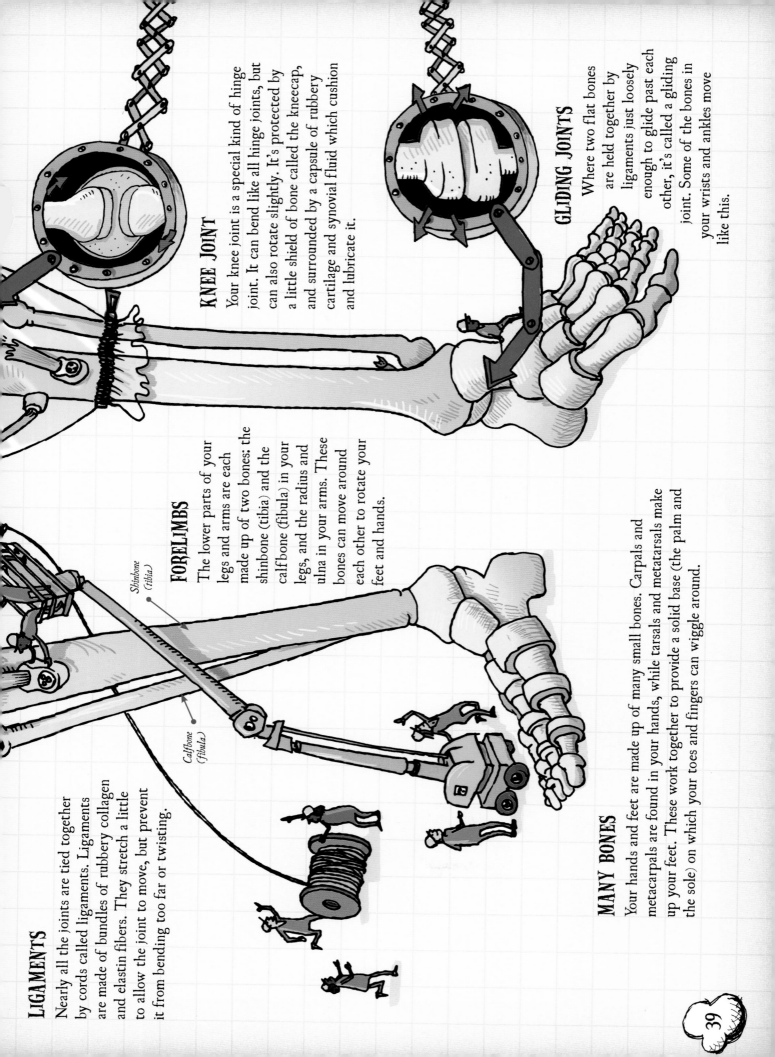

LIGAMENTS

Nearly all the joints are tied together by cords called ligaments. Ligaments are made of bundles of rubbery collagen and elastin fibers. They stretch a little to allow the joint to move, but prevent it from bending too far or twisting.

KNEE JOINT

Your knee joint is a special kind of hinge joint. It can bend like all hinge joints, but can also rotate slightly. It's protected by a little shield of bone called the kneecap, and surrounded by a capsule of rubbery cartilage and synovial fluid which cushion and lubricate it.

FORELIMBS

The lower parts of your legs and arms are each made up of two bones; the shinbone (tibia) and the calfbone (fibula) in your legs, and the radius and ulna in your arms. These bones can move around each other to rotate your feet and hands.

Shinbone (tibia)

Calfbone (fibula)

GLIDING JOINTS

Where two flat bones are held together by ligaments just loosely enough to glide past each other, it's called a gliding joint. Some of the bones in your wrists and ankles move like this.

MANY BONES

Your hands and feet are made up of many small bones. Carpals and metacarpals are found in your hands, while tarsals and metatarsals make up your feet. These work together to provide a solid base (the palm and the sole) on which your toes and fingers can wiggle around.

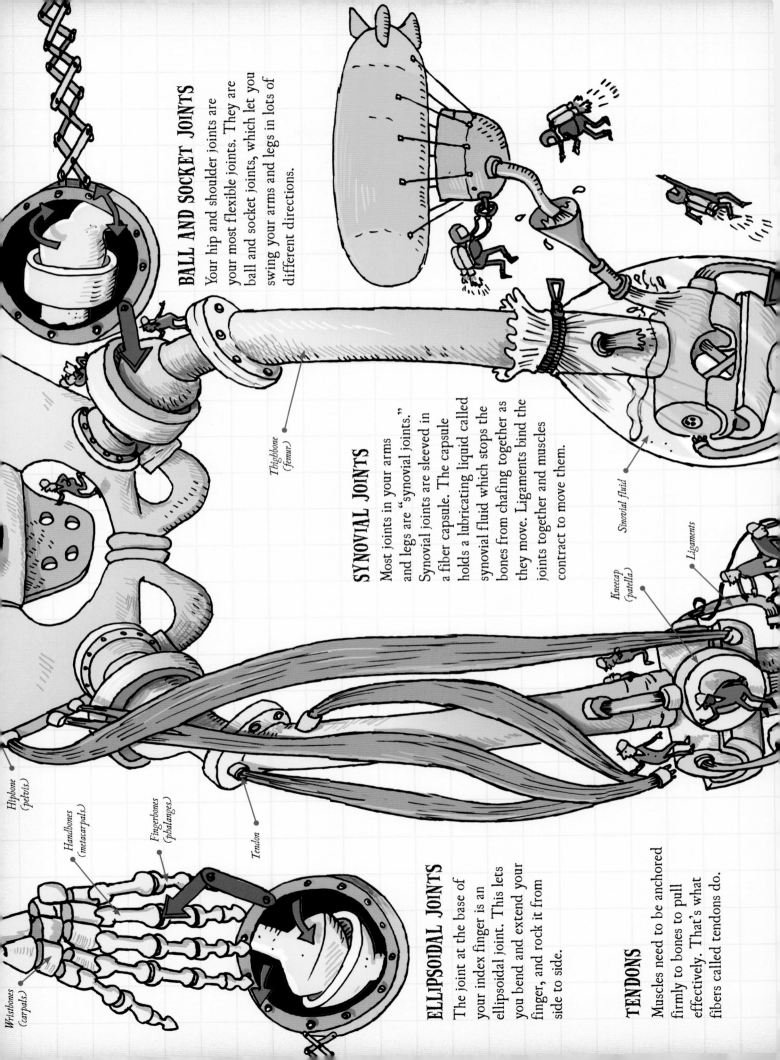

BALL AND SOCKET JOINTS

Your hip and shoulder joints are your most flexible joints. They are ball and socket joints, which let you swing your arms and legs in lots of different directions.

Thighbone (femur)

SYNOVIAL JOINTS

Most joints in your arms and legs are "synovial joints." Synovial joints are sleeved in a fiber capsule. The capsule holds a lubricating liquid called synovial fluid which stops the bones from chafing together as they move. Ligaments bind the joints together and muscles contract to move them.

Kneecap (patella)

Synovial fluid

Ligaments

Hipbone (pelvis)

Handbones (metacarpals)

Fingerbones (phalanges)

Tendon

Wristbones (carpals)

ELLIPSOIDAL JOINTS

The joint at the base of your index finger is an ellipsoidal joint. This lets you bend and extend your finger, and rock it from side to side.

TENDONS

Muscles need to be anchored firmly to bones to pull effectively. That's what fibers called tendons do.

HOW DO YOU GROW?

Your body is an amazing round-the-clock, cell-making machine. Every moment, it's making millions of new cells, as old ones die.

1. TIME FOR AN UPDATE

Most nerve cells last all your life, but skin cells last just a few weeks. On average, your entire set of body cells needs replacing every seven to ten years. You also need to replace any damaged cells.

2. GOING FOR GROWTH?

When you're young, you grow bigger every day. Your body does all this growing by making new cells. Sometimes you grow quickly, and sometimes slowly. But you only stop growing when you're an adult. Even then, your nose and ears go on growing.

STARTER CELLS

When your body began growing as an embryo (see page 76-77), it had all-purpose "stem" cells that divided to become all the different cells. Your body still has little pockets of stem cells that can be used to restock damaged or old cells.

BONE
BLOOD
STEM CELLS
LIVER
SKIN

3. DOUBLING UP

Your body can't build new cells from scratch. Instead, existing cells split in half, so each half becomes a new cell. When new cells are needed, cells go on dividing, creating more and more cells. This is called cell multiplication.

DNA copies itself

DNA

BLOOD
BONE

4. COPYCATS

All cells divide in the same way, so that new cells are exactly the same as the old ones. First the cell swells up. Then it copies its DNA, its program for life. All 23 pieces of DNA split in half lengthways to make two identical sets — one set for each new cell.

7. TIME TO DIE

A new cell knows it's in the right place if molecules on its surface match its neighbors. The molecules are its address label. But if the neighbors are different, the cell simply dies. Cells also self-destruct when damaged or worn out. This is called apoptosis and it helps protect your body from cancers.

6. THAT'S ENOUGH

When you're young, you need to grow more. So chemicals called cytokines trigger cells to divide faster. But when a cut is healed or a body part is fully grown, other cytokines tell cells to stop dividing.

8. GROWING BONES

Right now, your leg and arm bones are growing longer. Cells are dividing and multiplying at special "growth plates" on the ends of each bone. As new cells are added, the older ones are buried and turn into hard bone. When the bone has reached its full size, the growth plates seal over and turn to hard bone and you stop growing.

5. BREAKING UP

Once the cell has made sure its DNA is copied correctly, it sends one set to each end of the cell. Then the cell splits in half, and the membrane seals off each half to complete the new cells. This is called mitosis.

41

WHAT ARE HORMONES?

To adjust your body processes to suit your surroundings, or your time of life, you need chemical particles called hormones. Hormones move around in your blood and they tell cells what to do. When you're in a tight situation, a hormone called adrenaline gets your body ready for action.

HORMONE STORES

Hormone stores called glands are positioned around your body. They release hormones when they get the right trigger, which might be a change in your blood chemicals or another hormone.

PINEAL
controls your sleep patterns.

BRAIN
produces endorphin and enkephaline, which are your body's natural painkillers.

GROWTH HORMONE
boosts cell activity when you need to grow.

TSH
tells your thyroid gland to release the hormones that control how fast things happen in your body.

ADH
tells your body not to let too much water out in your urine.

FSH AND LH
tell a girl's ovaries (organs that hold egg cells) to swing into action.

ADRENALS
adrenaline and noradrenaline prepare your body for danger—fight or run away!

THYROID
thyroid hormones tell cells how fast to work.

PITUITARY GLAND

THYROID

THYROID
calcitonin controls how much calcium is in your blood.

PANCREAS
insulin and glucagon control sugar levels in your blood.

OVARIES (IN GIRLS)
estrogen and progesterone set your body's monthly cycle.

TESTES (IN BOYS)
testosterone affects your sex organs.

① AAGH! TIGER!
When you're in danger, your brain quickly sends out an emergency signal to the adrenal glands on top of your kidneys.

② FIGHT?
At once, the adrenals send out adrenaline and noradrenaline.

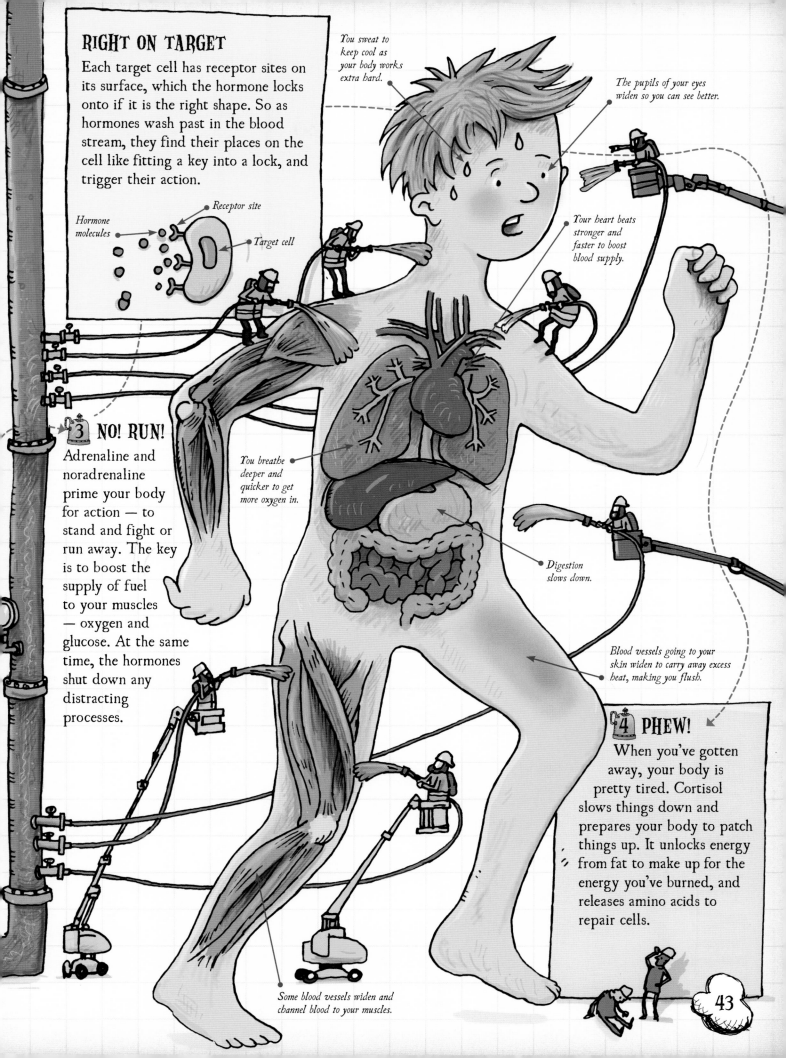

RIGHT ON TARGET

Each target cell has receptor sites on its surface, which the hormone locks onto if it is the right shape. So as hormones wash past in the blood stream, they find their places on the cell like fitting a key into a lock, and trigger their action.

Hormone molecules

Receptor site

Target cell

You sweat to keep cool as your body works extra hard.

The pupils of your eyes widen so you can see better.

Your heart beats stronger and faster to boost blood supply.

3 NO! RUN!

Adrenaline and noradrenaline prime your body for action — to stand and fight or run away. The key is to boost the supply of fuel to your muscles — oxygen and glucose. At the same time, the hormones shut down any distracting processes.

You breathe deeper and quicker to get more oxygen in.

Digestion slows down.

Blood vessels going to your skin widen to carry away excess heat, making you flush.

4 PHEW!

When you've gotten away, your body is pretty tired. Cortisol slows things down and prepares your body to patch things up. It unlocks energy from fat to make up for the energy you've burned, and releases amino acids to repair cells.

Some blood vessels widen and channel blood to your muscles.

WHAT DOES YOUR LIVER DO?

Your liver is a super-hot powerhouse of chemical activity. Day and night, it's busy working on 500 different chemical-processing tasks at once — purifying the blood, whipping the nutrients you absorbed in your blood into the right chemical shapes for the body to use, making bile to speed digestion, and much, much more.

Central vein

Hepatocytes

Branch of hepatic artery

LOBULE

Glucose

GLYCOGEN

GLYCOGEN

GLYCOGEN

GLYCOGEN

GLYCOGEN

GLYCOGEN

Sinusoid

4.> SWEET POWER

Lobules soon get busy turning carbohydrates from your food into glucose, the sugar that is your body's number one fuel. Some glucose goes straight into your blood to give your body cells the energy they need. But some is stored as glycogen — like energy bars ready in store for when you need a quick boost.

Blood vessel

LIVER

Hepatic artery

Portal vein

Bile duct

1.> LIVER DELIVER

Blood pours into the liver through two blood vessels: the hepatic artery and the portal vein. They enter through the big portal that runs up the middle.

Bile duct

Urea

Cholesterol

Lobule

2. MICROPROCESSING

From the portal, blood vessels spread out through the liver carrying blood directly to thousands of little processing units called lobules. Lobules are long and hexagonal, and split into wedges. Blood flows into each wedge through a channel called a sinusoid.

3. LIVER ACTION

In each sinusoid are the liver's special cells, the hepatocytes. As blood flows past them, they extract the right chemicals, such as carbohydrates and proteins, process them, and return them to the blood. Bile, though, is sent back out.

5. UREA OUT

When levels of unwanted proteins in your blood get too high, the liver turns them into a chemical called urea. The urea goes off in the blood to your kidneys for disposal in your pee — urea makes pee smelly as it turns into the gas ammonia.

6. FATS

Your liver takes fat that has been absorbed from your food into your blood and uses it to make cholesterol. Your body needs cholesterol to keep your cells sturdy — though too much can clog up your arteries when you get older.

7. FAT BREAKER

There's a third pipe passing through the portal. This is the bile duct. Bile is a green liquid your liver makes and sends off to your small intestine to help break down fatty food.

BILE

SOME OF THE LIVER'S MANY TASKS

· TURNING CARBOHYDRATES TO GLUCOSE
· STORING ENERGY IN THE FORM OF GLYCOGEN
· PACKING OFF EXCESS ENERGY FOR LONG-TERM STORAGE AS FAT
· CLEANING AWAY OLD BLOOD CELLS
· MAKING NEW BLOOD PLASMA PRODUCTS
· BREAKING DOWN WASTE PROTEINS
· TURNING FAT INTO CHOLESTEROL
· STORING VITAMINS

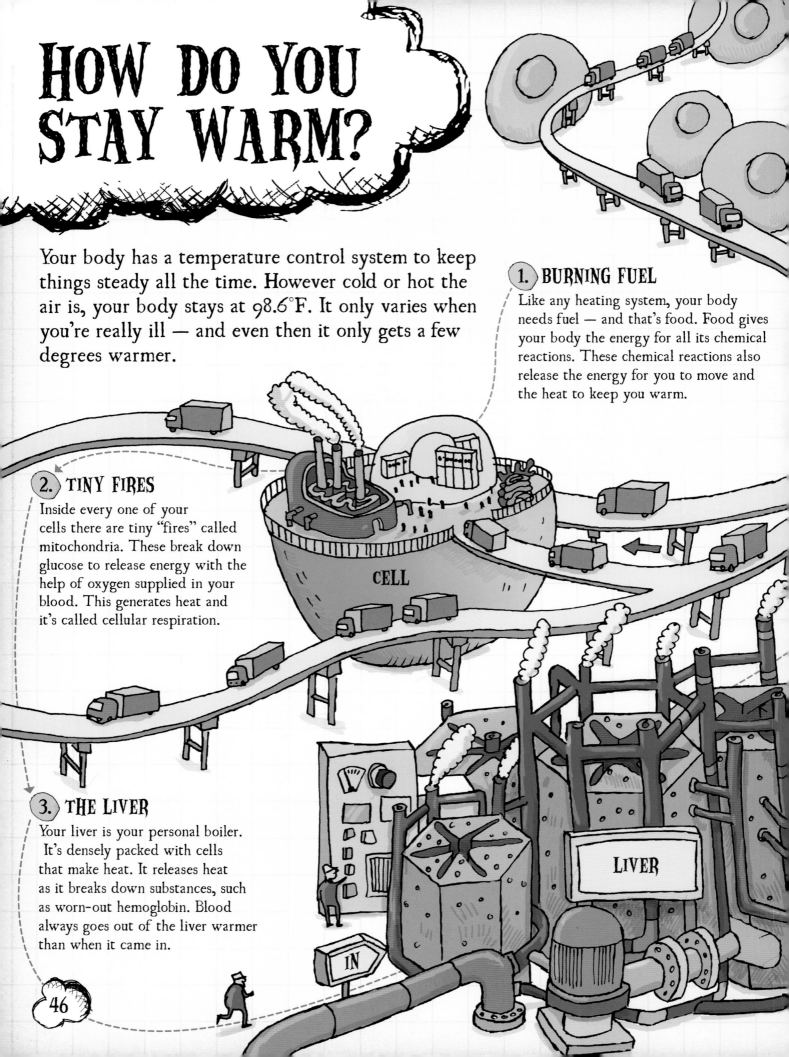

HOW DO YOU STAY WARM?

Your body has a temperature control system to keep things steady all the time. However cold or hot the air is, your body stays at 98.6°F. It only varies when you're really ill — and even then it only gets a few degrees warmer.

1. BURNING FUEL

Like any heating system, your body needs fuel — and that's food. Food gives your body the energy for all its chemical reactions. These chemical reactions also release the energy for you to move and the heat to keep you warm.

2. TINY FIRES

Inside every one of your cells there are tiny "fires" called mitochondria. These break down glucose to release energy with the help of oxygen supplied in your blood. This generates heat and it's called cellular respiration.

CELL

3. THE LIVER

Your liver is your personal boiler. It's densely packed with cells that make heat. It releases heat as it breaks down substances, such as worn-out hemoglobin. Blood always goes out of the liver warmer than when it came in.

IN

LIVER

COOLING DOWN

You constantly lose some heat through your skin and as you breathe out. But if you're still too hot, the body has several ways to cool down.

SWEAT IT OUT

If you're too hot, the hypothalamus tells your sweat glands to produce more sweat, which passes through pores in your skin. Sweating not only takes warm water out of your body, but also cools your skin as the sweat evaporates.

RED HOT

When you're hot, the hypothalamus also boosts the blood supply to your skin to take heat away from your body's core. Your skin glows bright red!

PANTS!

If you're really hot, you may pant. Panting is just breathing rapidly to blow heat out with your breath.

4. HOT OR COLD?

It's good to stay warm, but your body must not overheat. To make sure you don't get too hot or cold, there is a "thermostat" in your brain called the hypothalamus to monitor your temperature.

COLD HOT

BRAIN

WARMING UP

Your body has a number of techniques it can use to warm things up and to stop you from getting too chilly.

STOKE THOSE FIRES!

If you're too cold, the hypothalamus alerts your thyroid. The thyroid sends out hormones that boost cellular respiration to make more heat.

GOOSE BUMPS

If you're very cold, hairs on your skin may also stand up, giving you goose bumps. This may be a hangover from our hairier ancestors, since raising hairs trapped a layer of warm air next to the skin.

RESTRICTION

Your hypothalamus also sends signals to cut the supply of blood to your skin to keep any heat in your body's core. That's why you turn pale when you're cold.

GET MOVING!

In case that's not enough, the hypothalamus sends out nerve signals to make your muscles move rapidly. This is what's happening when you shiver.

OUT

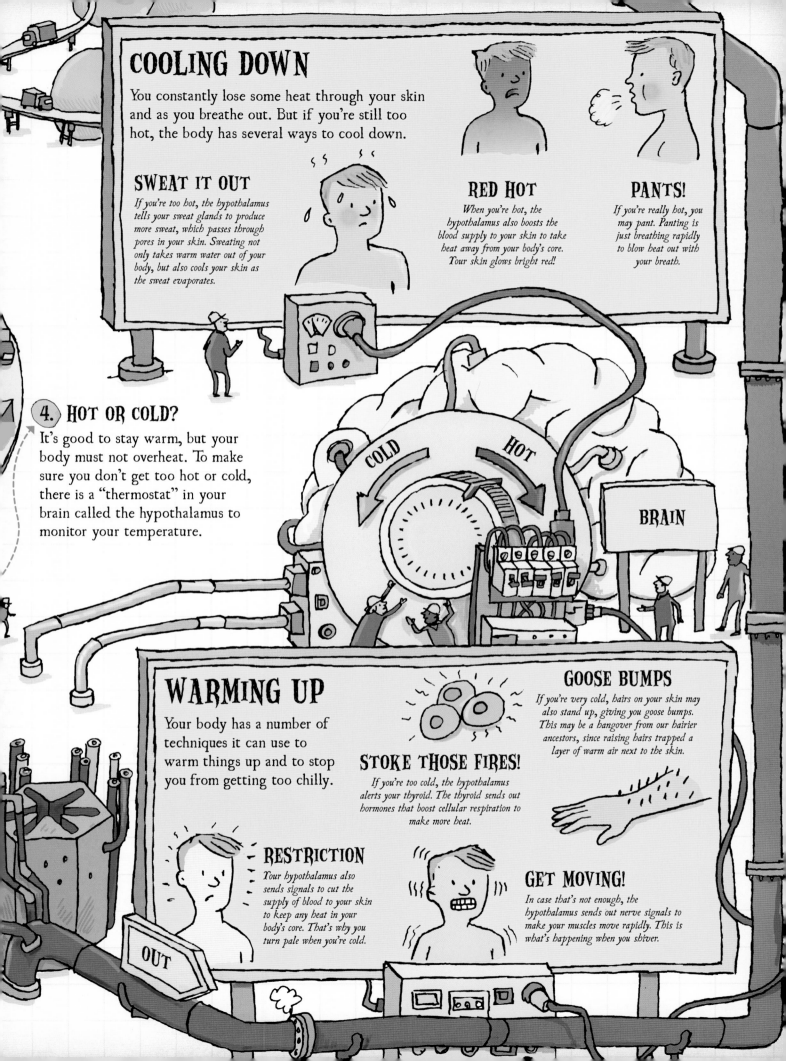

WHAT HAPPENS TO WATER?

Your body is more than 60 percent water. Water fills your cells, makes up most of your body fluids and keeps the chemistry of life going. Making sure your water levels are balanced is one of your kidneys' main jobs.

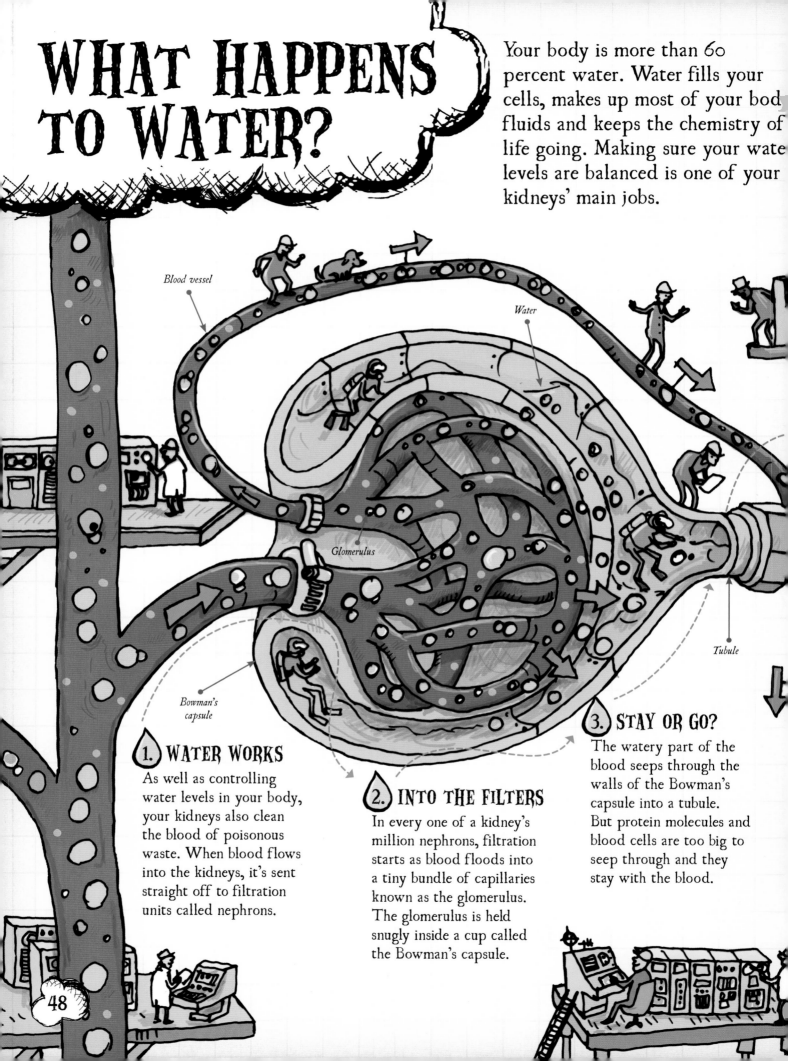

Blood vessel

Water

Glomerulus

Tubule

Bowman's capsule

1. WATER WORKS

As well as controlling water levels in your body, your kidneys also clean the blood of poisonous waste. When blood flows into the kidneys, it's sent straight off to filtration units called nephrons.

2. INTO THE FILTERS

In every one of a kidney's million nephrons, filtration starts as blood floods into a tiny bundle of capillaries known as the glomerulus. The glomerulus is held snugly inside a cup called the Bowman's capsule.

3. STAY OR GO?

The watery part of the blood seeps through the walls of the Bowman's capsule into a tubule. But protein molecules and blood cells are too big to seep through and they stay with the blood.

WHY DO YOU EAT?

Food is the fuel your body needs to keep going. It also provides the materials your body uses to grow and stay healthy. Unlike lions, which eat meat, and cows, which eat grass, we eat a range of foods, but they need to be in the right balance. These are the main food types you need.

START

BREAD

Brown whole-wheat bread gives you lots of fiber; white bread doesn't.

FRUIT AND VEGETABLES

Fruit and vegetables contain plenty of vitamins, but they don't contain everything your body needs, so vegetarians must be careful to eat the right mix.

VITAMINS

The smallest items on your "shopping" list are vitamins, known by the letters A to K. Vitamins are traces of chemicals your body needs but can't make itself. You can find each in particular foods, and each has a particular task in your body.

ROUGHAGE

To keep the muscles of your gut in tiptop condition, they need a good workout with "roughage." Roughage is cellulose plant fibers that are just too tough for your body to digest.

MEAT

Protein in meat contains all the amino acids your body needs. Meat is also rich in fats.

FISH

Fish are good sources of protein and vitamins.

PROTEINS

Your body needs proteins to provide the material to make and repair cells. The faster you grow, the more protein you need. Proteins are made from combinations of 20 different substances called amino acids. Your body can actually make 12 of these, but you have to get the others from your food.

WHERE DOES YOUR FOOD GO?

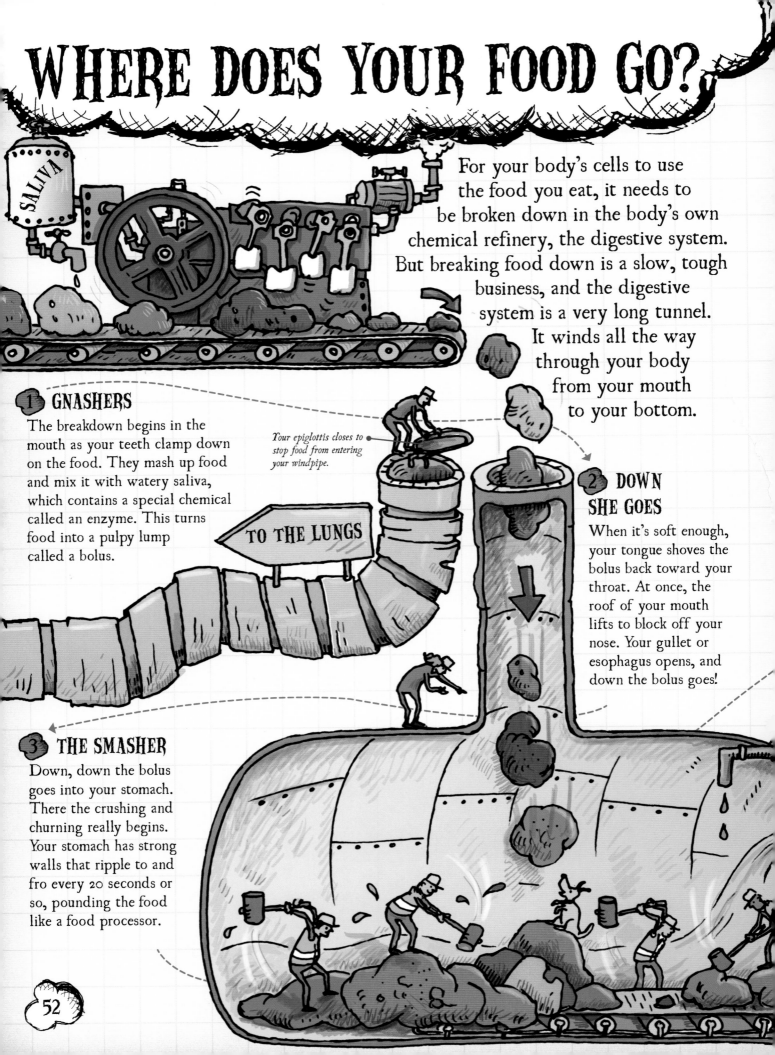

SALIVA

For your body's cells to use the food you eat, it needs to be broken down in the body's own chemical refinery, the digestive system. But breaking food down is a slow, tough business, and the digestive system is a very long tunnel. It winds all the way through your body from your mouth to your bottom.

1 GNASHERS

The breakdown begins in the mouth as your teeth clamp down on the food. They mash up food and mix it with watery saliva, which contains a special chemical called an enzyme. This turns food into a pulpy lump called a bolus.

Your epiglottis closes to stop food from entering your windpipe.

TO THE LUNGS

2 DOWN SHE GOES

When it's soft enough, your tongue shoves the bolus back toward your throat. At once, the roof of your mouth lifts to block off your nose. Your gullet or esophagus opens, and down the bolus goes!

3 THE SMASHER

Down, down the bolus goes into your stomach. There the crushing and churning really begins. Your stomach has strong walls that ripple to and fro every 20 seconds or so, pounding the food like a food processor.

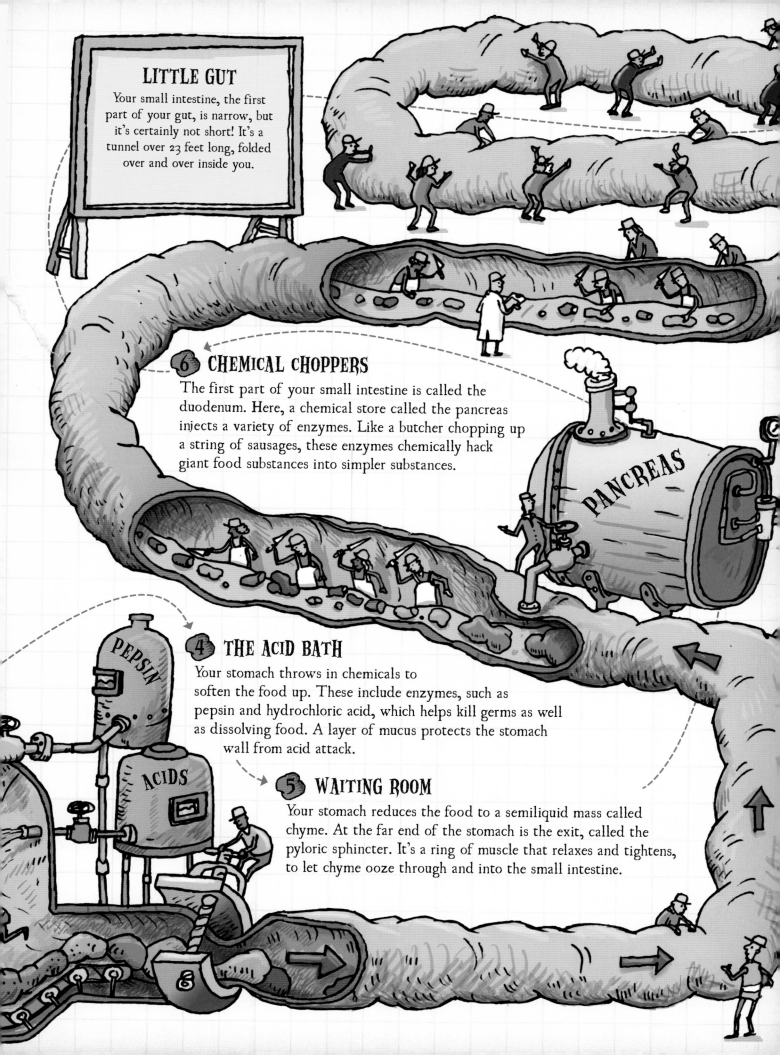

LITTLE GUT

Your small intestine, the first part of your gut, is narrow, but it's certainly not short! It's a tunnel over 23 feet long, folded over and over inside you.

6 CHEMICAL CHOPPERS

The first part of your small intestine is called the duodenum. Here, a chemical store called the pancreas injects a variety of enzymes. Like a butcher chopping up a string of sausages, these enzymes chemically hack giant food substances into simpler substances.

PANCREAS

4 THE ACID BATH

Your stomach throws in chemicals to soften the food up. These include enzymes, such as pepsin and hydrochloric acid, which helps kill germs as well as dissolving food. A layer of mucus protects the stomach wall from acid attack.

PEPSIN

ACIDS

5 WAITING ROOM

Your stomach reduces the food to a semiliquid mass called chyme. At the far end of the stomach is the exit, called the pyloric sphincter. It's a ring of muscle that relaxes and tightens, to let chyme ooze through and into the small intestine.

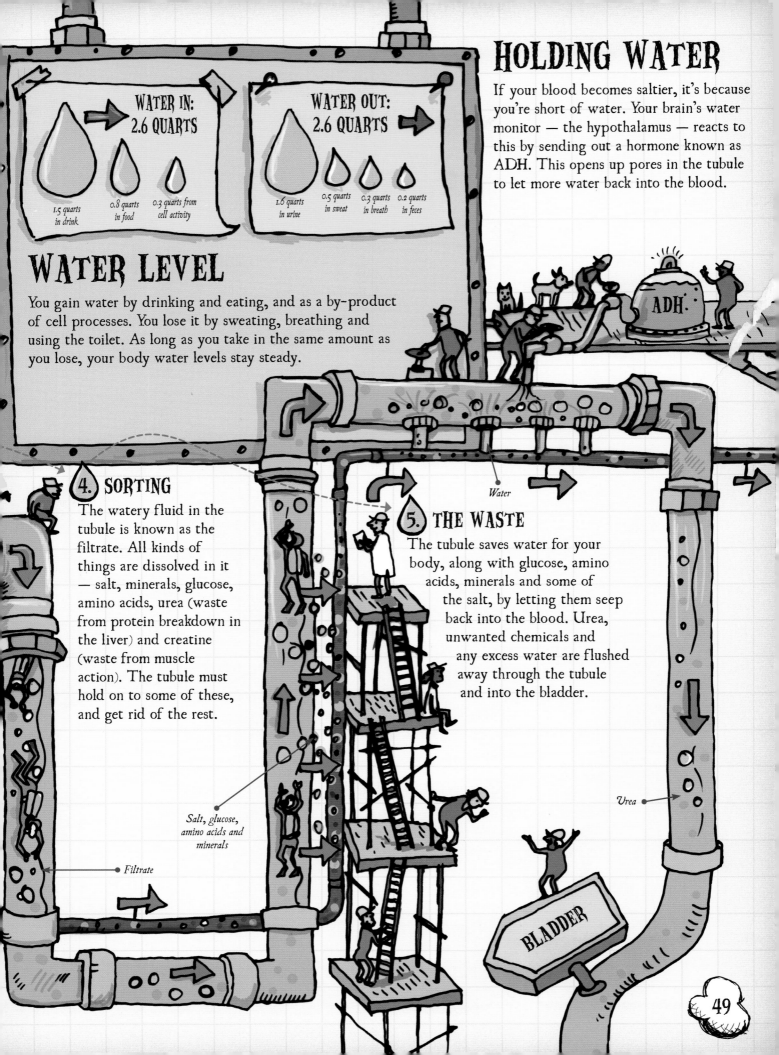

WATER IN:
2.6 QUARTS

1.5 quarts in drink

0.8 quarts in food

0.3 quarts from cell activity

WATER OUT:
2.6 QUARTS

1.6 quarts in urine

0.5 quarts in sweat

0.3 quarts in breath

0.2 quarts in feces

WATER LEVEL

You gain water by drinking and eating, and as a by-product of cell processes. You lose it by sweating, breathing and using the toilet. As long as you take in the same amount as you lose, your body water levels stay steady.

HOLDING WATER

If your blood becomes saltier, it's because you're short of water. Your brain's water monitor — the hypothalamus — reacts to this by sending out a hormone known as ADH. This opens up pores in the tubule to let more water back into the blood.

ADH.

Water

4. SORTING

The watery fluid in the tubule is known as the filtrate. All kinds of things are dissolved in it — salt, minerals, glucose, amino acids, urea (waste from protein breakdown in the liver) and creatine (waste from muscle action). The tubule must hold on to some of these, and get rid of the rest.

5. THE WASTE

The tubule saves water for your body, along with glucose, amino acids, minerals and some of the salt, by letting them seep back into the blood. Urea, unwanted chemicals and any excess water are flushed away through the tubule and into the bladder.

Salt, glucose, amino acids and minerals

Filtrate

Urea

BLADDER

49

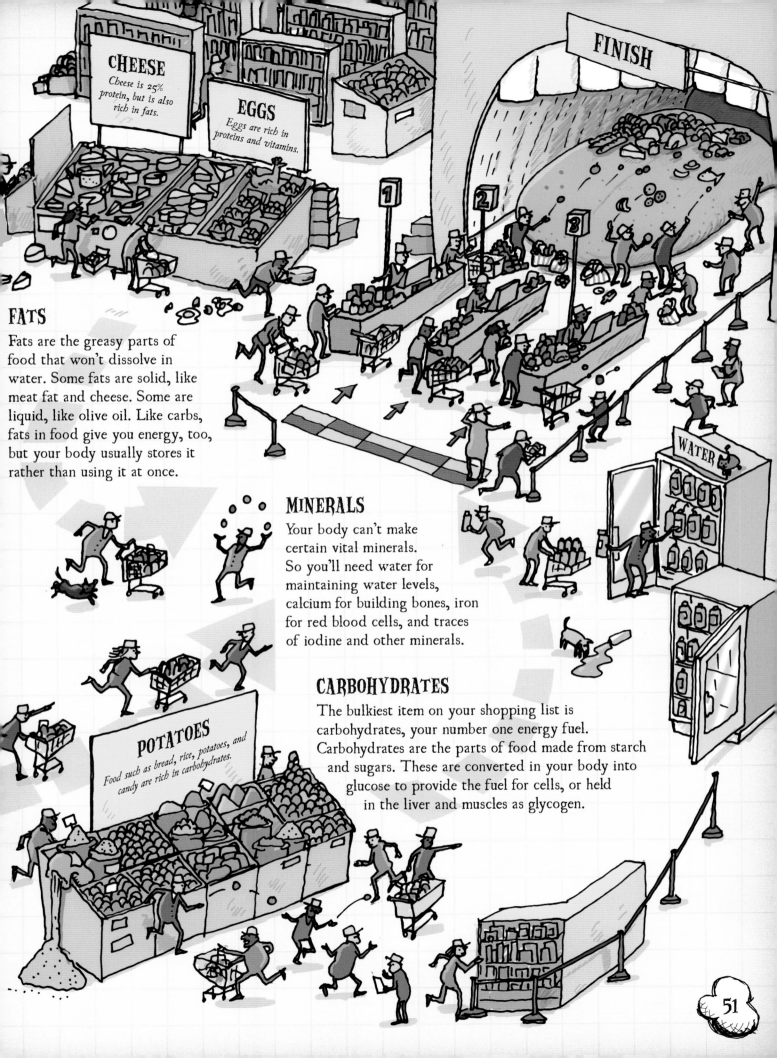

CHEESE
Cheese is 25% protein, but is also rich in fats.

EGGS
Eggs are rich in proteins and vitamins.

FINISH

FATS

Fats are the greasy parts of food that won't dissolve in water. Some fats are solid, like meat fat and cheese. Some are liquid, like olive oil. Like carbs, fats in food give you energy, too, but your body usually stores it rather than using it at once.

MINERALS

Your body can't make certain vital minerals. So you'll need water for maintaining water levels, calcium for building bones, iron for red blood cells, and traces of iodine and other minerals.

CARBOHYDRATES

The bulkiest item on your shopping list is carbohydrates, your number one energy fuel. Carbohydrates are the parts of food made from starch and sugars. These are converted in your body into glucose to provide the fuel for cells, or held in the liver and muscles as glycogen.

POTATOES
Food such as bread, rice, potatoes, and candy are rich in carbohydrates.

WATER

51

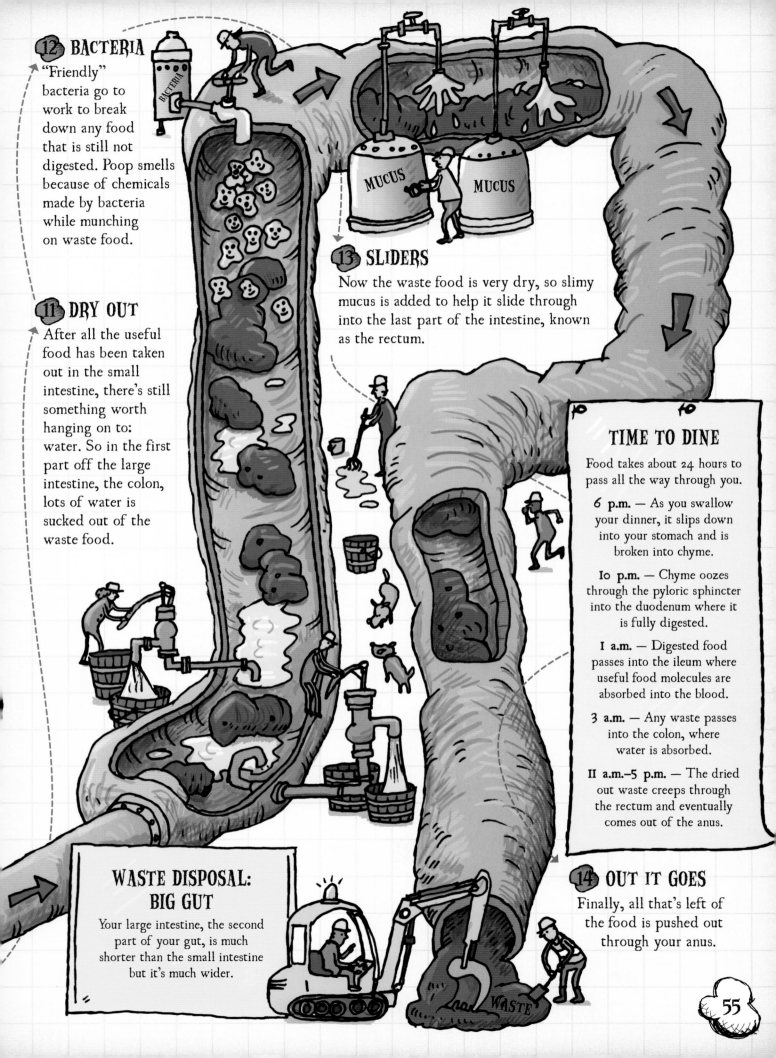

12 BACTERIA

"Friendly" bacteria go to work to break down any food that is still not digested. Poop smells because of chemicals made by bacteria while munching on waste food.

11 DRY OUT

After all the useful food has been taken out in the small intestine, there's still something worth hanging on to: water. So in the first part off the large intestine, the colon, lots of water is sucked out of the waste food.

13 SLIDERS

Now the waste food is very dry, so slimy mucus is added to help it slide through into the last part of the intestine, known as the rectum.

WASTE DISPOSAL: BIG GUT

Your large intestine, the second part of your gut, is much shorter than the small intestine but it's much wider.

TIME TO DINE

Food takes about 24 hours to pass all the way through you.

6 p.m. — As you swallow your dinner, it slips down into your stomach and is broken into chyme.

10 p.m. — Chyme oozes through the pyloric sphincter into the duodenum where it is fully digested.

1 a.m. — Digested food passes into the ileum where useful food molecules are absorbed into the blood.

3 a.m. — Any waste passes into the colon, where water is absorbed.

11 a.m.–5 p.m. — The dried out waste creeps through the rectum and eventually comes out of the anus.

14 OUT IT GOES

Finally, all that's left of the food is pushed out through your anus.

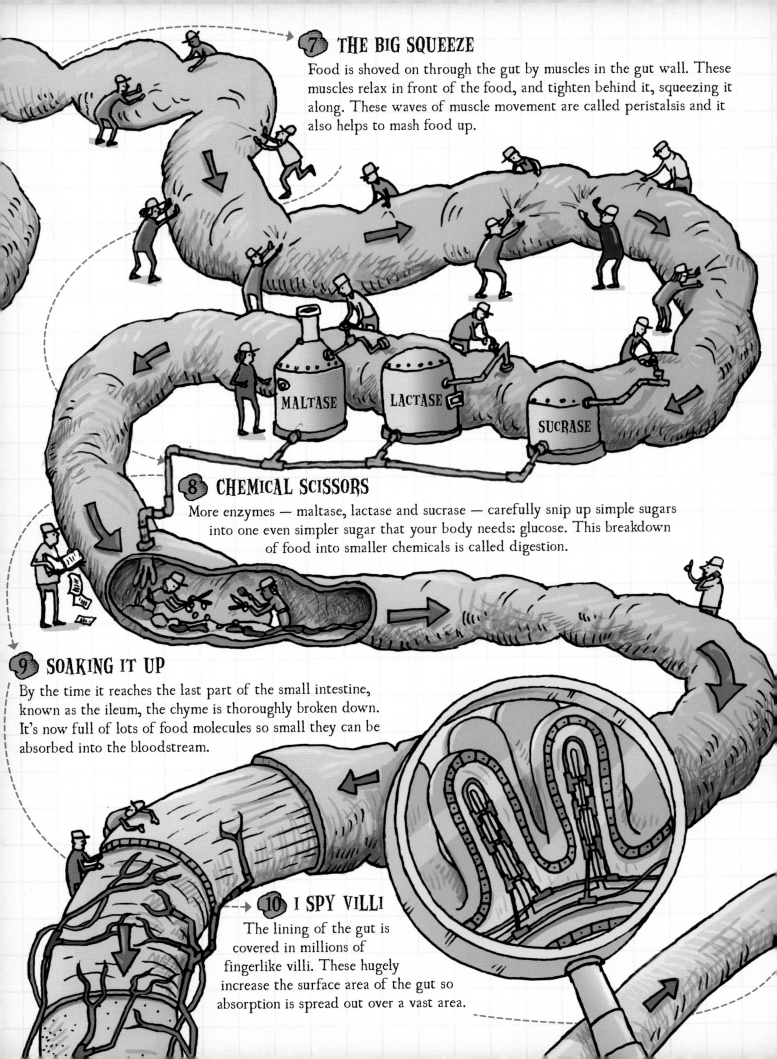

7 THE BIG SQUEEZE

Food is shoved on through the gut by muscles in the gut wall. These muscles relax in front of the food, and tighten behind it, squeezing it along. These waves of muscle movement are called peristalsis and it also helps to mash food up.

MALTASE

LACTASE

SUCRASE

8 CHEMICAL SCISSORS

More enzymes — maltase, lactase and sucrase — carefully snip up simple sugars into one even simpler sugar that your body needs: glucose. This breakdown of food into smaller chemicals is called digestion.

9 SOAKING IT UP

By the time it reaches the last part of the small intestine, known as the ileum, the chyme is thoroughly broken down. It's now full of lots of food molecules so small they can be absorbed into the bloodstream.

10 I SPY VILLI

The lining of the gut is covered in millions of fingerlike villi. These hugely increase the surface area of the gut so absorption is spread out over a vast area.

WHAT ARE NERVES?

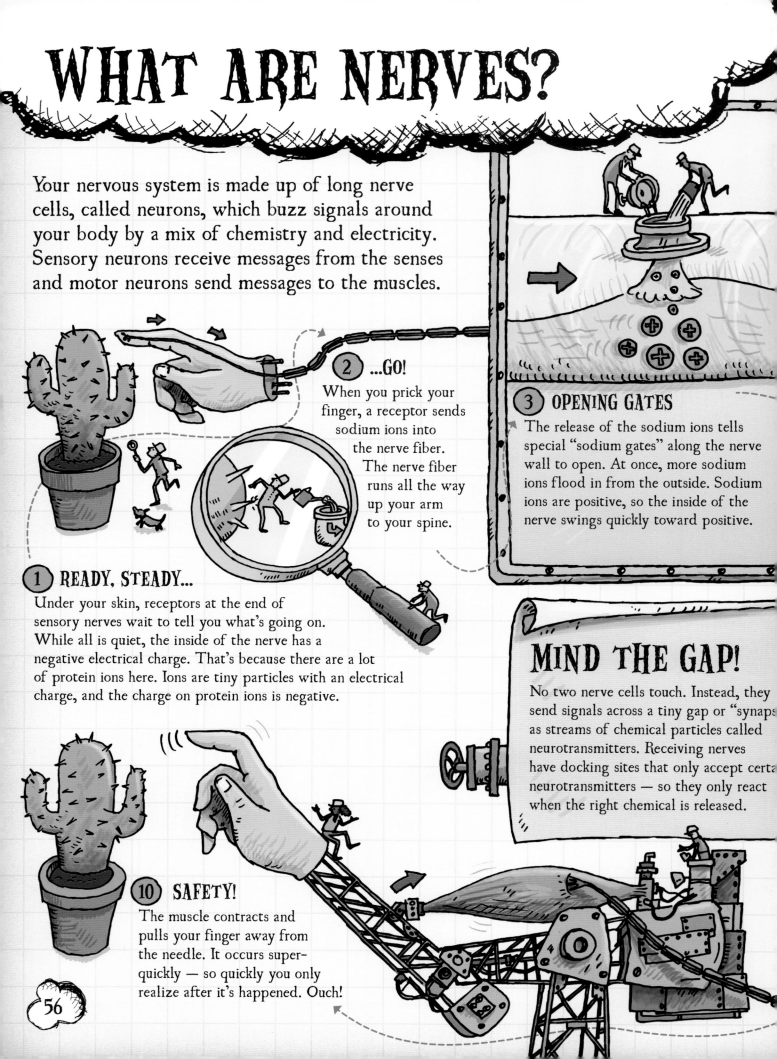

Your nervous system is made up of long nerve cells, called neurons, which buzz signals around your body by a mix of chemistry and electricity. Sensory neurons receive messages from the senses and motor neurons send messages to the muscles.

2 ...GO!

When you prick your finger, a receptor sends sodium ions into the nerve fiber. The nerve fiber runs all the way up your arm to your spine.

3 OPENING GATES

The release of the sodium ions tells special "sodium gates" along the nerve wall to open. At once, more sodium ions flood in from the outside. Sodium ions are positive, so the inside of the nerve swings quickly toward positive.

1 READY, STEADY...

Under your skin, receptors at the end of sensory nerves wait to tell you what's going on. While all is quiet, the inside of the nerve has a negative electrical charge. That's because there are a lot of protein ions here. Ions are tiny particles with an electrical charge, and the charge on protein ions is negative.

MIND THE GAP!

No two nerve cells touch. Instead, they send signals across a tiny gap or "synapse" as streams of chemical particles called neurotransmitters. Receiving nerves have docking sites that only accept certain neurotransmitters — so they only react when the right chemical is released.

10 SAFETY!

The muscle contracts and pulls your finger away from the needle. It occurs super-quickly — so quickly you only realize after it's happened. Ouch!

ots of muscle movements in your body happen without you thinking about them, as in this case. They are called reflexes and they let your body react to a hazard lightning fast before it gets damaged.

⑤ BACK TO NEGATIVE

Potassium gates open behind the impulse and let out positive potassium ions. This keeps the signal short and the inside of the nerve becomes negative again.

⑥ RESET

In time, a third set of gates will open to let potassium ions drift back in and sodium ions drift back out, so that the nerve is ready to send another signal.

④ MAGNETIC WAVE

Because unlike electrical charges attract each other, the positive sodium ions are tugged rapidly up the nerve fiber where it's still mostly negative. As they whoosh on, they trigger more sodium gates to open at lightning speed.

⑦ SPINE

The signal quickly reaches your spine, where the sensory nerve connects to other nerves along branches called dendrites. Through these, the signal passes on to nerves that go all the way up to your brain to tell you you're hurt.

Neurotransmitters

⑧ EMERGENCY SIGNAL

Because your finger could get damaged, the sensory nerve also buzzes directly to a motor nerve via a link called an interneuron.

Docking site

Receiving nerve

⑨ TELLING MUSCLES

When the motor nerve gets that pain signal from the interneuron, it zaps an impulse down toward the muscles that move your finger.

Interneuron

TO THE BRAIN

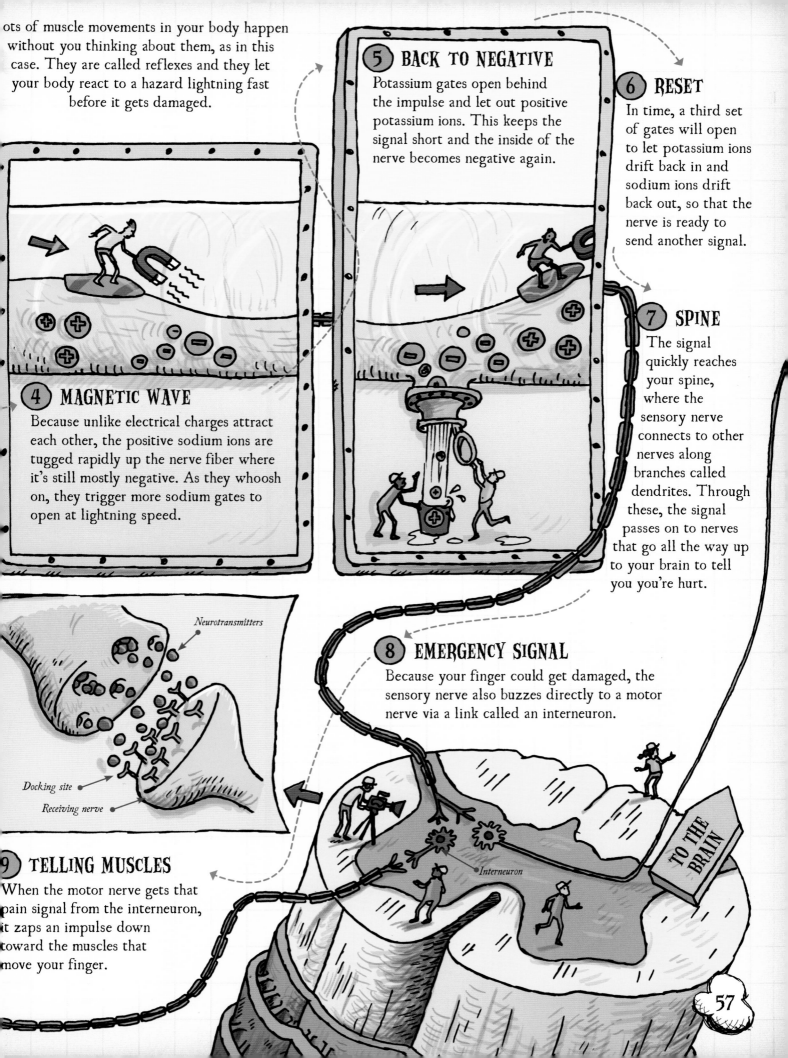

57

HOW DO YOU SEE?

Each of your eyes is an amazing camera with a powerful built-in lens that captures a fantastically clear picture of the world. Behind your eyes, your brain has a clever visual processing system to make instant sense of the picture.

1. LIGHT ENTERS THE EYE

Light enters your eyes through your cornea, which bends the rays of light from the object you are viewing. The light then passes through a small lens that adjusts the focus to produce a sharp picture, whether you are looking close up or far away.

2. DARK PORTHOLE

Between the cornea and the lens, light passes through the pupil, the dark hole in the center of your eyes. It looks black because your eye is dark inside. The colored ring around it is the iris. When light is dim, tiny muscles pull the iris wide open to let more light in.

4. NIGHT AND DAY

Your retina has two kinds of light-sensitive cell: rods and cones. There are 150 million rods that detect if it's dark or light, and work in very low light. Eight million cones identify colors and work best in daylight.

3. MOVIE TIME

The lenses focus an image onto the retina at the back of your eye. This image is just a fraction of an inch across, yet to your brain it seems so big and real that you never think of it as a picture at all.

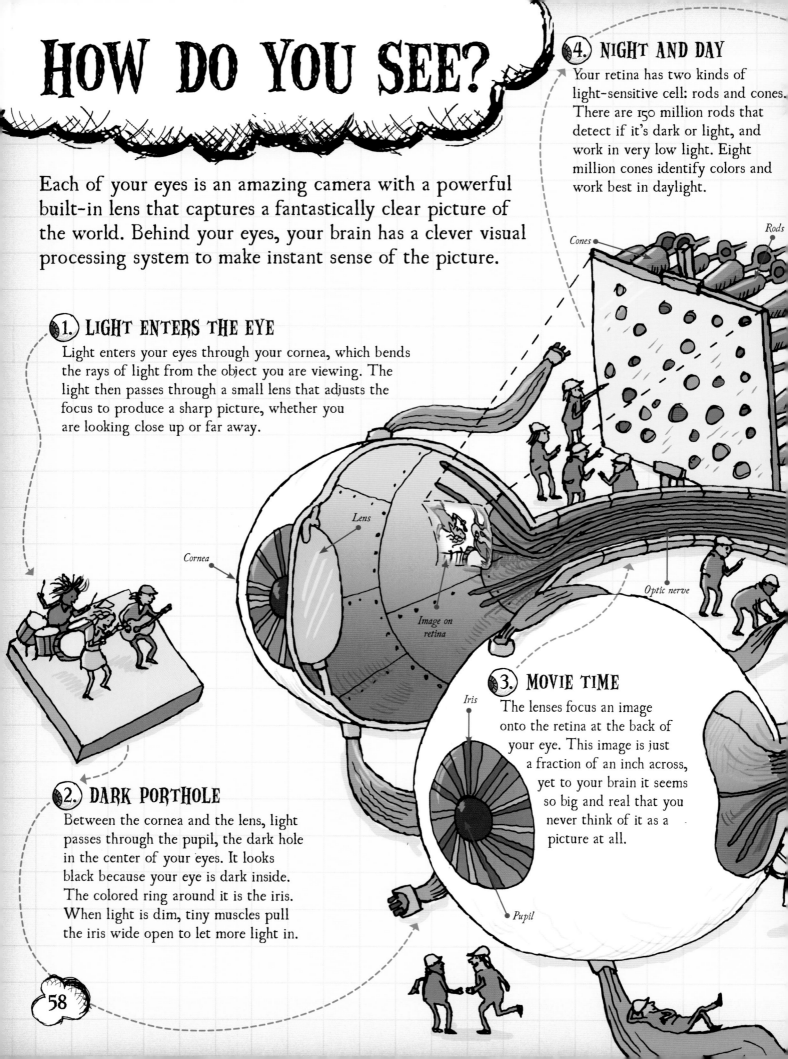

Cones

Rods

Cornea

Lens

Image on retina

Optic nerve

Iris

Pupil

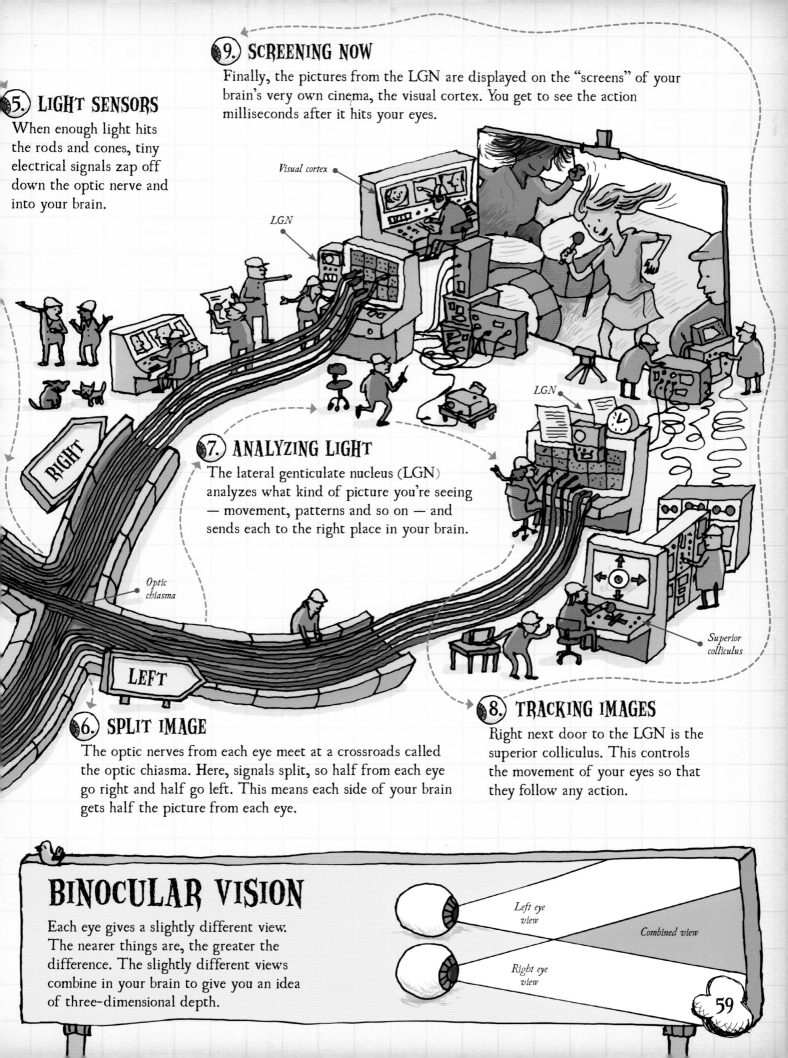

5. LIGHT SENSORS

When enough light hits the rods and cones, tiny electrical signals zap off down the optic nerve and into your brain.

9. SCREENING NOW

Finally, the pictures from the LGN are displayed on the "screens" of your brain's very own cinema, the visual cortex. You get to see the action milliseconds after it hits your eyes.

Visual cortex

LGN

LGN

7. ANALYZING LIGHT

The lateral geniculate nucleus (LGN) analyzes what kind of picture you're seeing — movement, patterns and so on — and sends each to the right place in your brain.

RIGHT

Optic chiasma

LEFT

Superior colliculus

6. SPLIT IMAGE

The optic nerves from each eye meet at a crossroads called the optic chiasma. Here, signals split, so half from each eye go right and half go left. This means each side of your brain gets half the picture from each eye.

8. TRACKING IMAGES

Right next door to the LGN is the superior colliculus. This controls the movement of your eyes so that they follow any action.

BINOCULAR VISION

Each eye gives a slightly different view. The nearer things are, the greater the difference. The slightly different views combine in your brain to give you an idea of three-dimensional depth.

Left eye view

Combined view

Right eye view

59

HOW DO YOUR EARS WORK?

Sounds are really just vibrations in the air, big or small, fast or slow. When a guitar string twangs, you can often actually see the movement that sets the air vibrating to and fro. But it's the same with other sounds. Your ears are just fantastically sensitive machines designed to detect these invisible vibrations*.

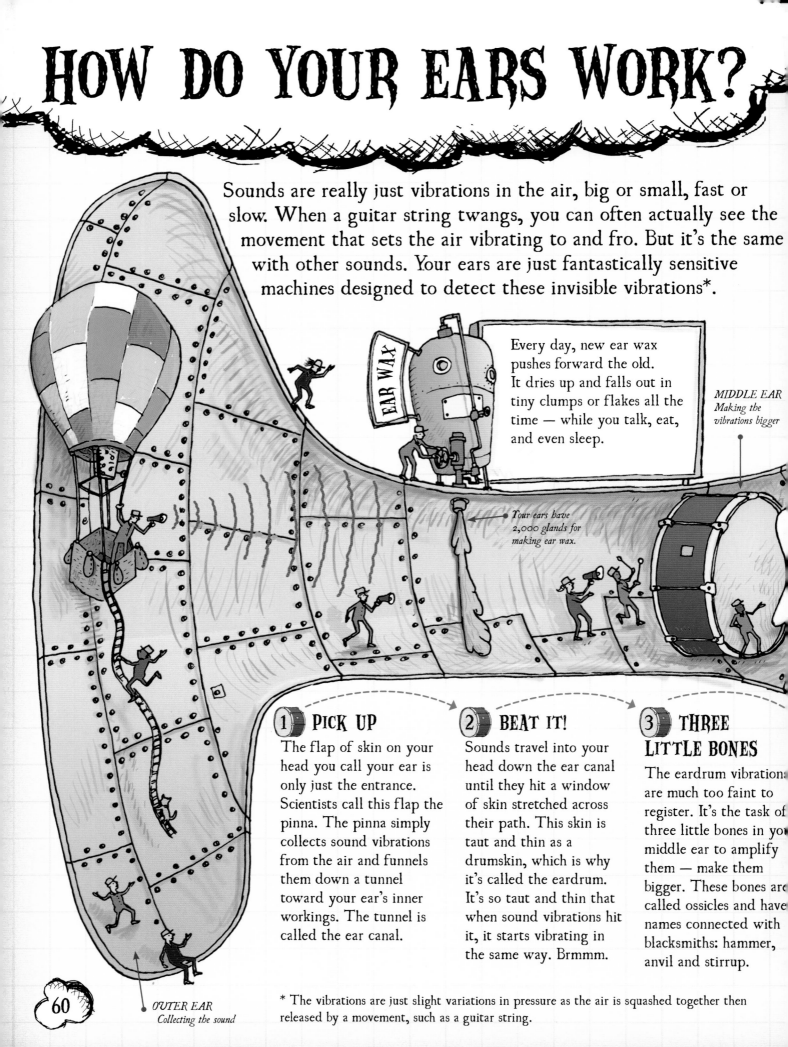

EAR WAX

Every day, new ear wax pushes forward the old. It dries up and falls out in tiny clumps or flakes all the time — while you talk, eat, and even sleep.

MIDDLE EAR
Making the vibrations bigger

Your ears have 2,000 glands for making ear wax.

OUTER EAR
Collecting the sound

1 PICK UP

The flap of skin on your head you call your ear is only just the entrance. Scientists call this flap the pinna. The pinna simply collects sound vibrations from the air and funnels them down a tunnel toward your ear's inner workings. The tunnel is called the ear canal.

2 BEAT IT!

Sounds travel into your head down the ear canal until they hit a window of skin stretched across their path. This skin is taut and thin as a drumskin, which is why it's called the eardrum. It's so taut and thin that when sound vibrations hit it, it starts vibrating in the same way. Brmmm.

3 THREE LITTLE BONES

The eardrum vibrations are much too faint to register. It's the task of three little bones in your middle ear to amplify them — make them bigger. These bones are called ossicles and have names connected with blacksmiths: hammer, anvil and stirrup.

* The vibrations are just slight variations in pressure as the air is squashed together then released by a movement, such as a guitar string.

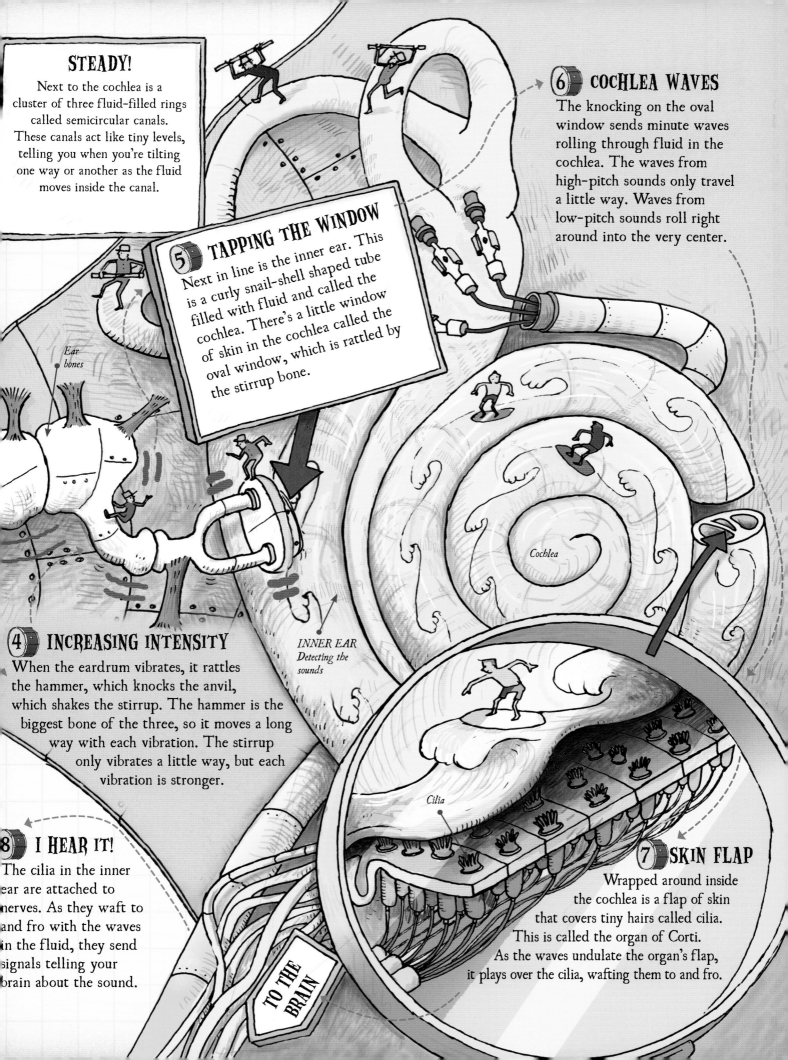

STEADY!

Next to the cochlea is a cluster of three fluid-filled rings called semicircular canals. These canals act like tiny levels, telling you when you're tilting one way or another as the fluid moves inside the canal.

6 COCHLEA WAVES

The knocking on the oval window sends minute waves rolling through fluid in the cochlea. The waves from high-pitch sounds only travel a little way. Waves from low-pitch sounds roll right around into the very center.

5 TAPPING THE WINDOW

Next in line is the inner ear. This is a curly snail-shell shaped tube filled with fluid and called the cochlea. There's a little window of skin in the cochlea called the oval window, which is rattled by the stirrup bone.

Ear bones

INNER EAR Detecting the sounds

Cochlea

4 INCREASING INTENSITY

When the eardrum vibrates, it rattles the hammer, which knocks the anvil, which shakes the stirrup. The hammer is the biggest bone of the three, so it moves a long way with each vibration. The stirrup only vibrates a little way, but each vibration is stronger.

8 I HEAR IT!

The cilia in the inner ear are attached to nerves. As they waft to and fro with the waves in the fluid, they send signals telling your brain about the sound.

Cilia

7 SKIN FLAP

Wrapped around inside the cochlea is a flap of skin that covers tiny hairs called cilia. This is called the organ of Corti. As the waves undulate the organ's flap, it plays over the cilia, wafting them to and fro.

TO THE BRAIN

HOW DO YOU SMELL AND TASTE?

Your nose is a remarkable chemical-detecting device. It can identify over 3,000 different chemicals from the vapor they give off. It can detect just a few tiny particles from among billions in the air. Your tongue is a chemical detector, too. You get the taste of food from your nose and tongue together.

1. THE OLFACTORY

Inside the top of your nose is a tiny patch of smell sensors called the olfactory epithelium. Each of the sensors in the lining of the nose has its own hairlike antenna that sticks a little way into the air current and picks up smell molecules.

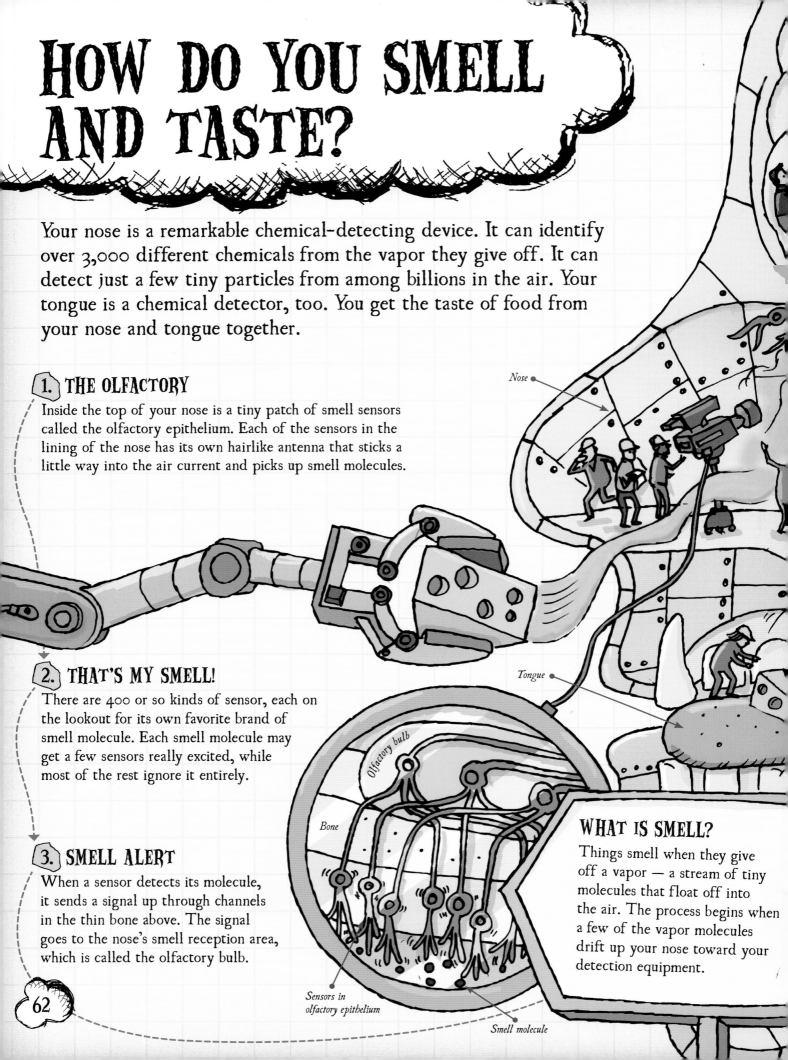

Nose

Tongue

2. THAT'S MY SMELL!

There are 400 or so kinds of sensor, each on the lookout for its own favorite brand of smell molecule. Each smell molecule may get a few sensors really excited, while most of the rest ignore it entirely.

Olfactory bulb

Bone

3. SMELL ALERT

When a sensor detects its molecule, it sends a signal up through channels in the thin bone above. The signal goes to the nose's smell reception area, which is called the olfactory bulb.

WHAT IS SMELL?

Things smell when they give off a vapor — a stream of tiny molecules that float off into the air. The process begins when a few of the vapor molecules drift up your nose toward your detection equipment.

Sensors in olfactory epithelium

Smell molecule

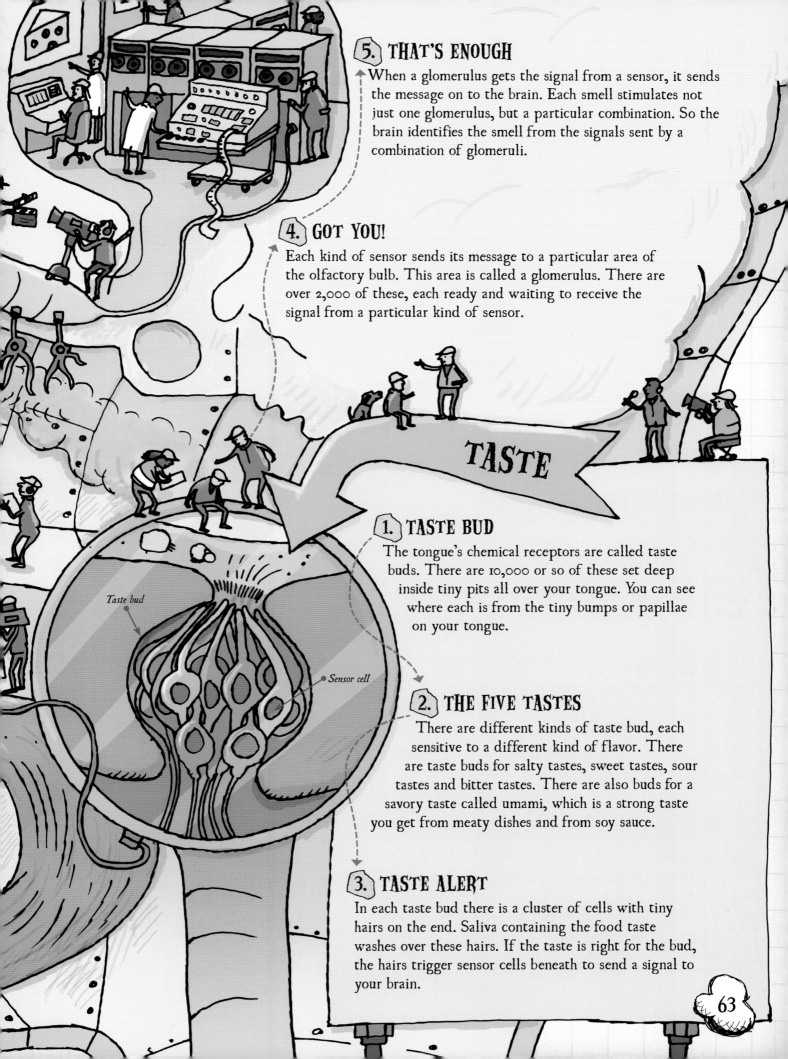

5. THAT'S ENOUGH

When a glomerulus gets the signal from a sensor, it sends the message on to the brain. Each smell stimulates not just one glomerulus, but a particular combination. So the brain identifies the smell from the signals sent by a combination of glomeruli.

4. GOT YOU!

Each kind of sensor sends its message to a particular area of the olfactory bulb. This area is called a glomerulus. There are over 2,000 of these, each ready and waiting to receive the signal from a particular kind of sensor.

TASTE

Taste bud

Sensor cell

1. TASTE BUD

The tongue's chemical receptors are called taste buds. There are 10,000 or so of these set deep inside tiny pits all over your tongue. You can see where each is from the tiny bumps or papillae on your tongue.

2. THE FIVE TASTES

There are different kinds of taste bud, each sensitive to a different kind of flavor. There are taste buds for salty tastes, sweet tastes, sour tastes and bitter tastes. There are also buds for a savory taste called umami, which is a strong taste you get from meaty dishes and from soy sauce.

3. TASTE ALERT

In each taste bud there is a cluster of cells with tiny hairs on the end. Saliva containing the food taste washes over these hairs. If the taste is right for the bud, the hairs trigger sensor cells beneath to send a signal to your brain.

63

HOW DO YOU THINK?

Your brain is an amazing computer. It is made from nearly 100 billion nerve cells. Each one makes thousands of connections with others, so there are trillions of alternative routes for nerve signals. It's all these connections that make you think and make you smart.

MAKING YOUR MIND UP

Your brain is actually 85 percent water and quite a lot of fat. But what really matters is all the nerve cells that are held in tight bundles by supporting cells. All your thoughts come as signals that whizz through this amazing network.

TWO HALVES

Your brain is split into two halves, or hemispheres, linked by a bundle of nerves. Some people believe the left side tends to deal with things in a more logical, detailed way, while the right has a more emotional overview.

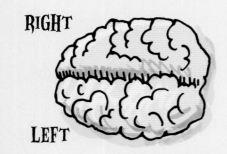

RIGHT

LEFT

THOUGHT SO

Thoughts are nerve signals that buzz through the brain and make you talk and think, laugh and cry, love and hate, and do everything else that makes you who you are. What you're thinking depends on which nerve pathways fire up. Pathways that get used a lot get stronger and quicker. Those that are hardly used tend to get lost.

LEFT HEMISPHERE (OUTSIDE)

SENSORY CORTEX

Sensing the skin – pain, heat, touch and other things

BROCA'S AREA

Controls what you say

AUDITORY CORTEX

Where you interpret sounds

FRONTAL LOBE

Where you decide what to do and where to move

TEMPORAL LOBE

Imagination, intelligence, emotion and language

THINKING ABOUT IT?

The wrinkled outer layer, or cortex, is where conscious thoughts go on. These are thoughts you know about. There are other subconscious thoughts going on deep inside your brain that you know very little about!

RIGHT HEMISPHERE (INSIDE)

SMELL CENTER

Processing what you smell

AMYGDALA

The amygdala controls emotions and helps you make decisions.

HOW DO YOU GET SICK?

It's not fun when you're sick. Sometimes the problem is internal, such as cancer. More often, though, the problem comes from outside. Your body comes under attack by microbes, such as viruses. Most of the time your body can fight these off, but sometimes they make you sick.

Most microbes spread through the air in sneezes, coughs, or even just breathing.

BACTERIA

Bacteria are by far the most common microbe. There are many thousands of different kinds. But they are all made from just one cell, and they can multiply very rapidly.

SPIRILLA

Spirilla look like tiny spiral noodles. They come in badly cooked shellfish and stale drinking water, and they cause diarrhea and stomach upsets.

COCCI

Cocci are plump, round bacteria. They often they live up your nose harmlessly — which means they are easily spread. But they can cause some very nasty diseases, including pneumonia, scarlet fever and meningitis.

BACILLI

Bacilli are long and thin, like rods. They cause terrible diseases, such as tetanus, typhoid, tuberculosis (TB), whooping cough and diphtheria. Not welcome!

Germs can spread in food, too, especially uncooked food.

AWFUL ORGANICS

You can also be made sick by fungi spores and by small protozoa.

66

HOW DO YOU GET BETTER?

When your body comes under attack from germs, it defends itself with a series of weapons known as the immune system. It's so clever that scientists are only just beginning to understand how it all works.

1 SKIN TIGHT

Skin is your first line of defense. Skin cells are so closely knitted together that not even bacteria can slip in between! Glands ooze sebum, an oil that keeps your skin moist and stops it from cracking. It's also slightly acidic, which some bacteria don't like. Germs may also be crowded out by friendly bacteria.

Germs that try to sneak in through your nose may get caught in mucus or sneezed out.

Germs that hide away in your food may get vomited out.

Sebum

OUTER DEFENSES
Like a fortress, your body has lots of barriers and booby traps to stop germs even getting in.

RAPID REACTION
Sometimes, germs such as viruses get inside your body to start their nasty work. At once, your inner defenses kick off with the Innate System. It's not particularly clever, and it targets every intruder in the same rough way. But it gets into action super-fast.

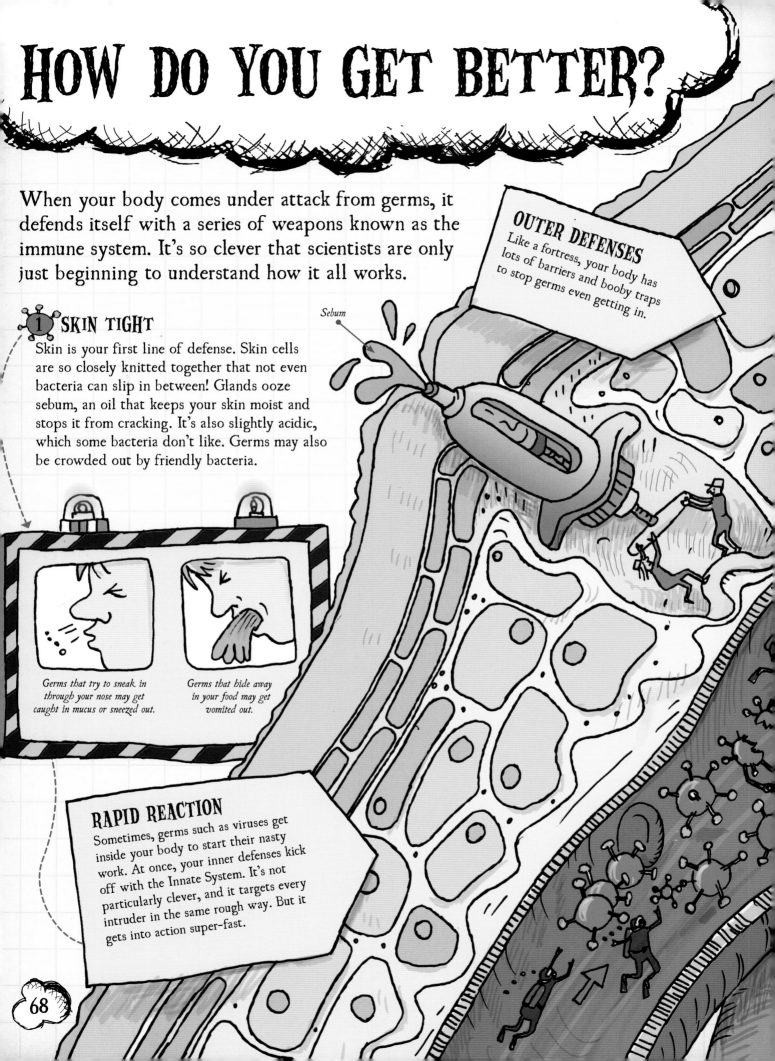

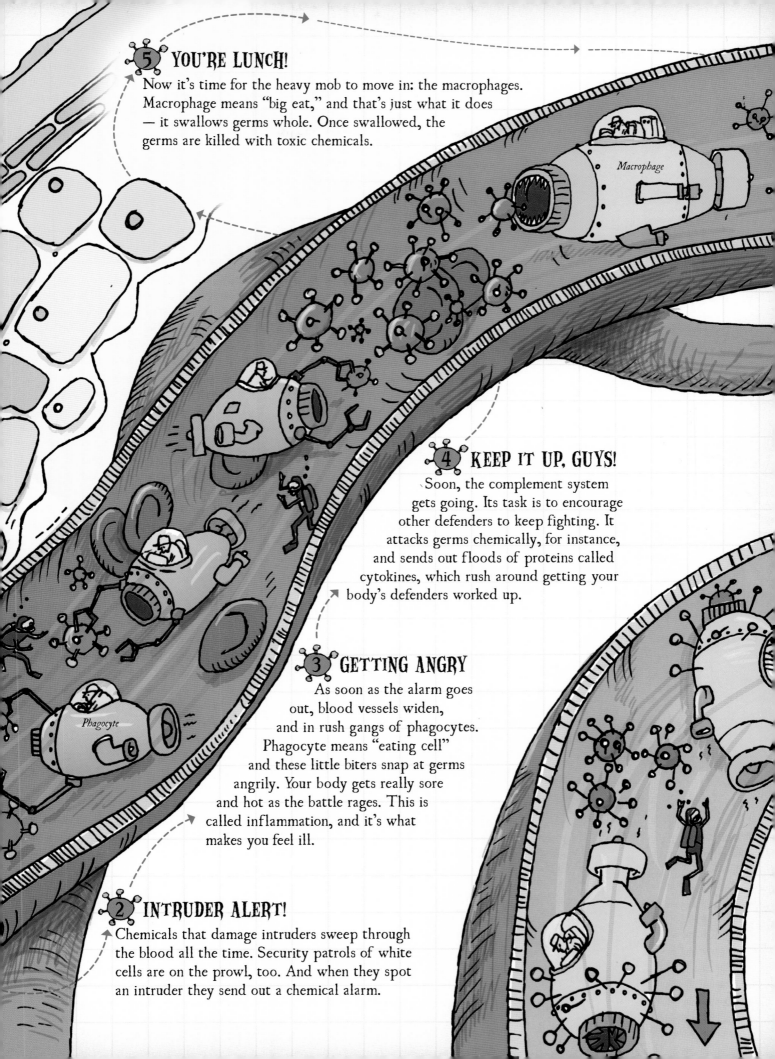

5 YOU'RE LUNCH!

Now it's time for the heavy mob to move in: the macrophages. Macrophage means "big eat," and that's just what it does — it swallows germs whole. Once swallowed, the germs are killed with toxic chemicals.

Macrophage

4 KEEP IT UP, GUYS!

Soon, the complement system gets going. Its task is to encourage other defenders to keep fighting. It attacks germs chemically, for instance, and sends out floods of proteins called cytokines, which rush around getting your body's defenders worked up.

3 GETTING ANGRY

As soon as the alarm goes out, blood vessels widen, and in rush gangs of phagocytes. Phagocyte means "eating cell" and these little biters snap at germs angrily. Your body gets really sore and hot as the battle rages. This is called inflammation, and it's what makes you feel ill.

Phagocyte

2 INTRUDER ALERT!

Chemicals that damage intruders sweep through the blood all the time. Security patrols of white cells are on the prowl, too. And when they spot an intruder they send out a chemical alarm.

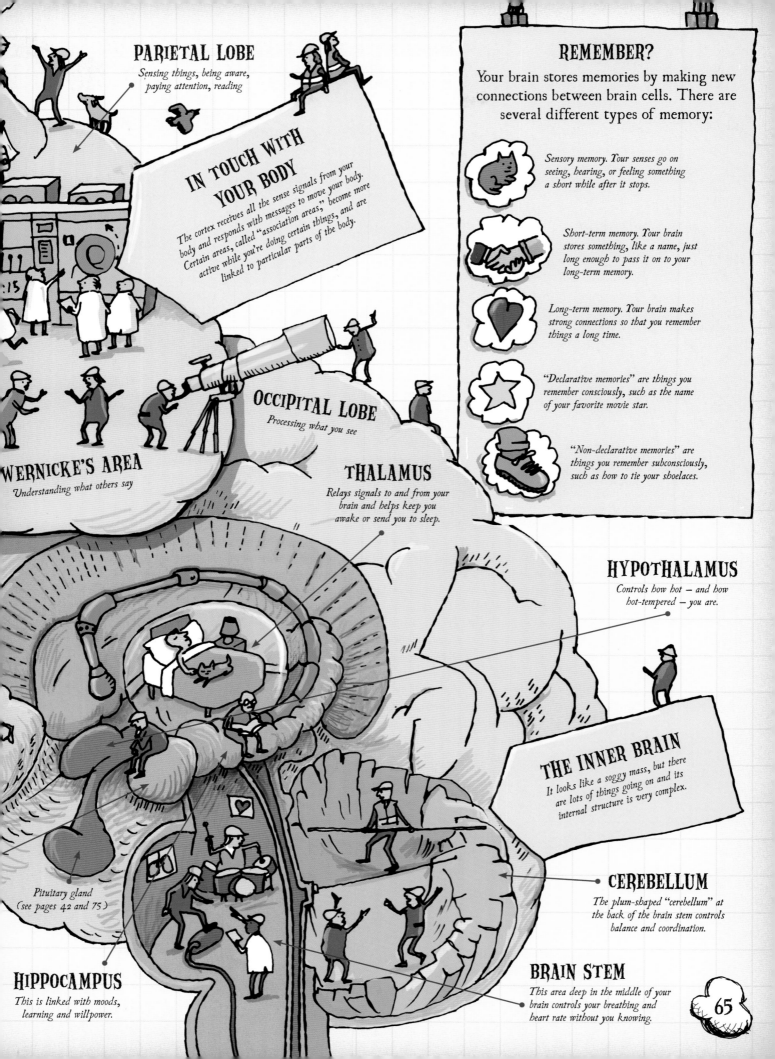

PARIETAL LOBE
Sensing things, being aware, paying attention, reading

IN TOUCH WITH YOUR BODY
The cortex receives all the sense signals from your body and responds with messages to move your body. Certain areas, called "association areas," become more active while you're doing certain things, and are linked to particular parts of the body.

OCCIPITAL LOBE
Processing what you see

WERNICKE'S AREA
Understanding what others say

THALAMUS
Relays signals to and from your brain and helps keep you awake or send you to sleep.

REMEMBER?
Your brain stores memories by making new connections between brain cells. There are several different types of memory:

Sensory memory. Your senses go on seeing, hearing, or feeling something a short while after it stops.

Short-term memory. Your brain stores something, like a name, just long enough to pass it on to your long-term memory.

Long-term memory. Your brain makes strong connections so that you remember things a long time.

"Declarative memories" are things you remember consciously, such as the name of your favorite movie star.

"Non-declarative memories" are things you remember subconsciously, such as how to tie your shoelaces.

HYPOTHALAMUS
Controls how hot — and how hot-tempered — you are.

THE INNER BRAIN
It looks like a soggy mass, but there are lots of things going on and its internal structure is very complex.

CEREBELLUM
The plum-shaped "cerebellum" at the back of the brain stem controls balance and coordination.

HIPPOCAMPUS
This is linked with moods, learning and willpower.

Pituitary gland
(see pages 42 and 75)

BRAIN STEM
This area deep in the middle of your brain controls your breathing and heart rate without you knowing.

65

WHY DO YOU LOOK LIKE YOUR MOM AND DAD?

You probably look a bit like your mom and dad. That's because you were made using the same recipe, or genes. You're basically a mix of your mom's and your dad's genes. But you have got a few that are just yours, created by tiny random changes called mutations.

1. THE AMAZING DOUBLE SPIRA

Inside each of your cells is a tangled chemical called DNA. DNA is made from two long strands twisted into a double spiral or "helix," like a twisted rope ladder.

2. RUNGS

Chemicals called bases run along each DNA strand. Each joins with a base on the other strand to make the ladder's rungs. There are four kinds of base — guanine, adenine, cytosine and thymine.

3. MATCHING BASES

Guanine only ever joins with cytosine, and adenine only with thymine. So the sequence of bases along each of the two strands must match. That means each strand can be used to make a copy of the other.

4. THE GENETIC CODE

The bases give a code for making chemicals called amino acids. Each base is like a letter and they come in groups of three, making words called codons. Each codon is the code for a particular amino acid.

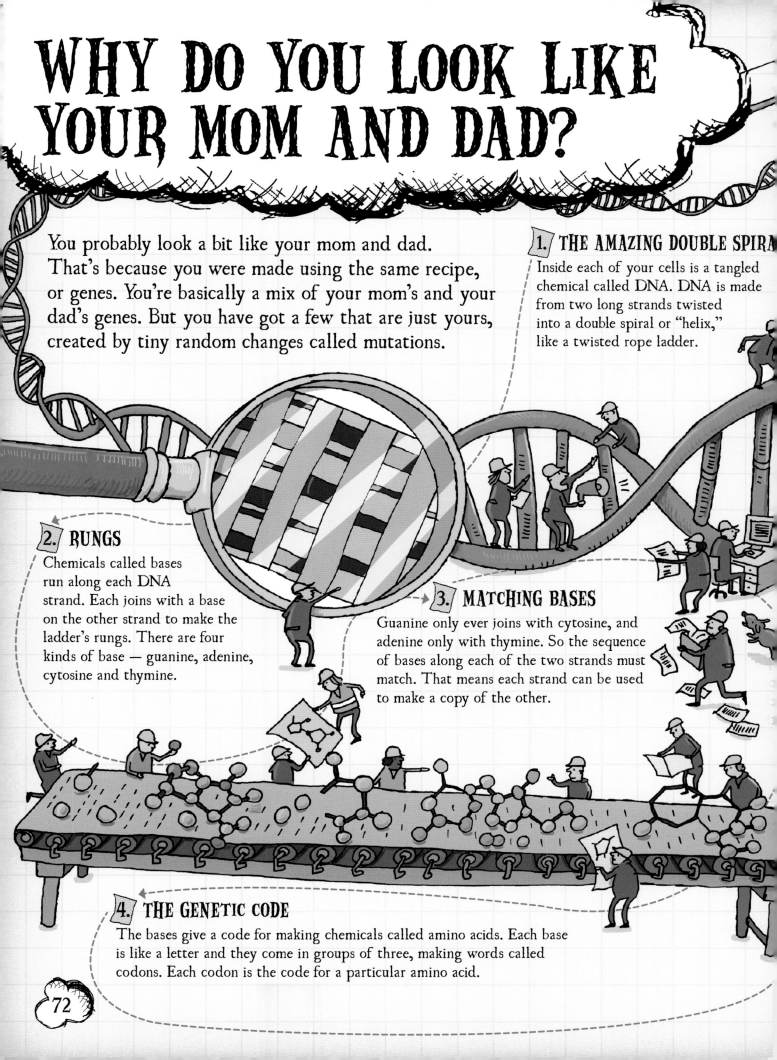

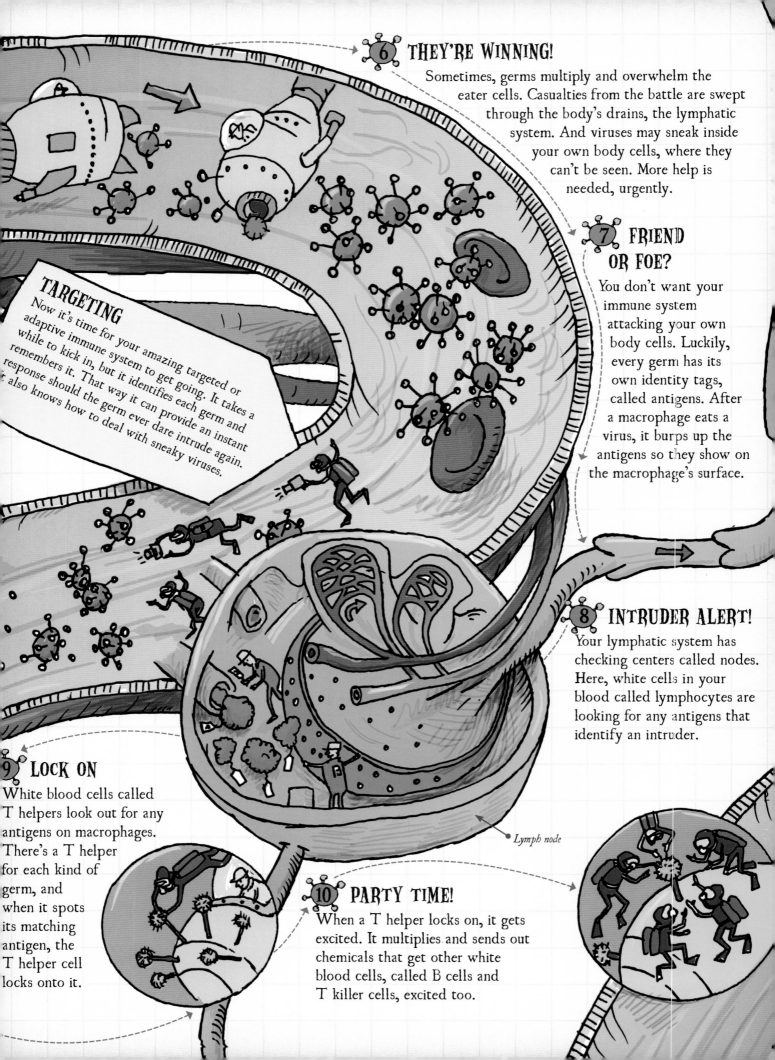

6 THEY'RE WINNING!

Sometimes, germs multiply and overwhelm the eater cells. Casualties from the battle are swept through the body's drains, the lymphatic system. And viruses may sneak inside your own body cells, where they can't be seen. More help is needed, urgently.

7 FRIEND OR FOE?

You don't want your immune system attacking your own body cells. Luckily, every germ has its own identity tags, called antigens. After a macrophage eats a virus, it burps up the antigens so they show on the macrophage's surface.

TARGETING

Now it's time for your amazing targeted or adaptive immune system to get going. It takes a while to kick in, but it identifies each germ and remembers it. That way it can provide an instant response should the germ ever dare intrude again. It also knows how to deal with sneaky viruses.

8 INTRUDER ALERT!

Your lymphatic system has checking centers called nodes. Here, white cells in your blood called lymphocytes are looking for any antigens that identify an intruder.

Lymph node

9 LOCK ON

White blood cells called T helpers look out for any antigens on macrophages. There's a T helper for each kind of germ, and when it spots its matching antigen, the T helper cell locks onto it.

10 PARTY TIME!

When a T helper locks on, it gets excited. It multiplies and sends out chemicals that get other white blood cells, called B cells and T killer cells, excited too.

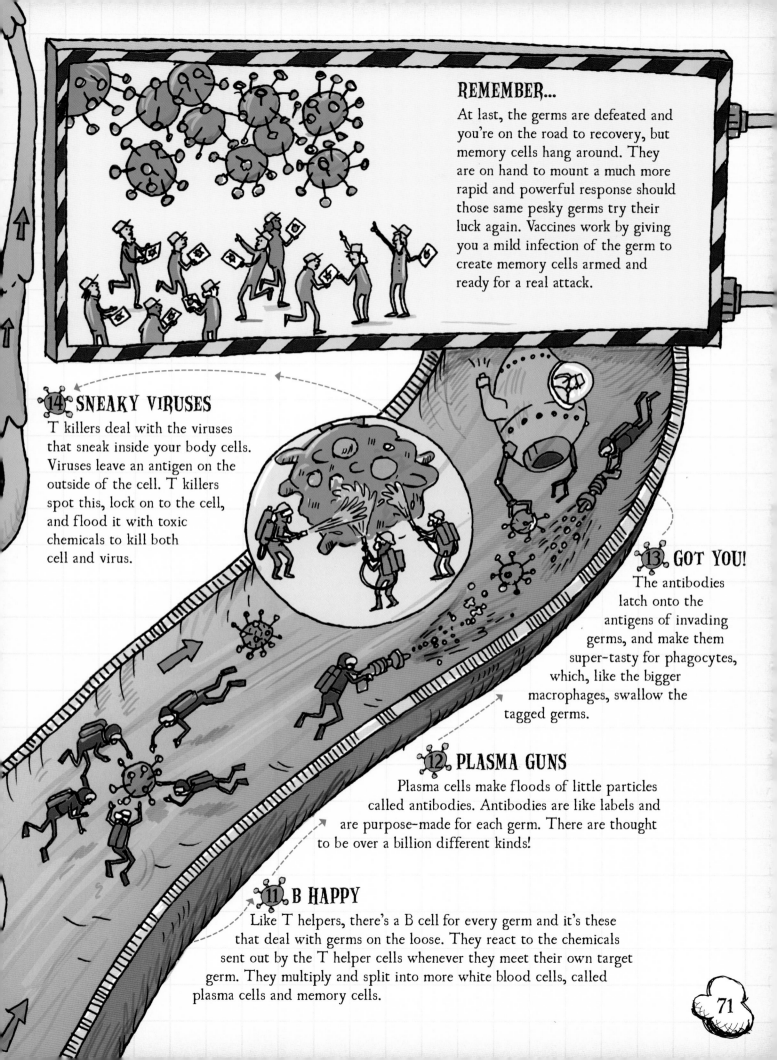

REMEMBER...

At last, the germs are defeated and you're on the road to recovery, but memory cells hang around. They are on hand to mount a much more rapid and powerful response should those same pesky germs try their luck again. Vaccines work by giving you a mild infection of the germ to create memory cells armed and ready for a real attack.

14 SNEAKY VIRUSES

T killers deal with the viruses that sneak inside your body cells. Viruses leave an antigen on the outside of the cell. T killers spot this, lock on to the cell, and flood it with toxic chemicals to kill both cell and virus.

13 GOT YOU!

The antibodies latch onto the antigens of invading germs, and make them super-tasty for phagocytes, which, like the bigger macrophages, swallow the tagged germs.

12 PLASMA GUNS

Plasma cells make floods of little particles called antibodies. Antibodies are like labels and are purpose-made for each germ. There are thought to be over a billion different kinds!

11 B HAPPY

Like T helpers, there's a B cell for every germ and it's these that deal with germs on the loose. They react to the chemicals sent out by the T helper cells whenever they meet their own target germ. They multiply and split into more white blood cells, called plasma cells and memory cells.

VIRUSES

Bacteria are tiny, but viruses are even tinier and can only be seen with powerful microscopes. In fact, they can't live by themselves. They survive and multiply only by taking over other cells.

RUBELLA

Rubella or German measles is caused by a virus known as the togavirus. It's spread through droplets of moisture from the nose or throat of someone who's infected, just like a cold.

INFLUENZA

Influenza viruses give you colds and flu. Like master criminals, they come in so many disguises that it's hard to keep track. There's more than 500 kinds with new ones popping up all the time.

Germs can also spread in sweat, saliva and blood.

ADENOVIRUS

Adenoviruses can infect your lungs and give you coughs. They sneak into your eyes, causing conjunctivitis. They even get right into your guts and give you diarrhea.

HIV

Human Immunodeficiency Virus (HIV) is to blame for the terrible disease AIDS. It makes your immune system actually attack your body rather than fight disease. AIDS stands for Acquired Immune Deficiency Syndrome.

Some germs are spread by contact. You might pick them up by touching a surface that someone with the germs has touched.

PARASITE PESTS

Parasites, such as tapeworms, are animals that move in and try to live off your body.

WHY DO I FEEL SO BAD?

Germs can damage your body by releasing toxins or disturbing body processes. When germs invade, your body starts to fight them off. Many of the nasty symptoms, such as fever and aching joints, are the side effects of the fight rather than a direct effect of the germ itself.

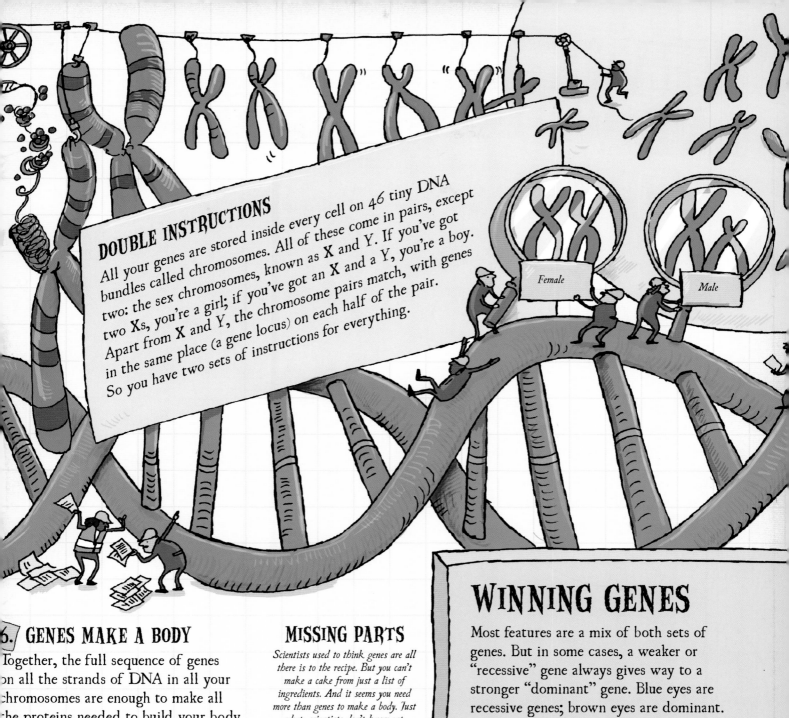

All your genes are stored inside every cell on 46 tiny DNA bundles called chromosomes. All of these come in pairs, except two: the sex chromosomes, known as X and Y. If you've got two Xs, you're a girl; if you've got an X and a Y, you're a boy. Apart from X and Y, the chromosome pairs match, with genes in the same place (a gene locus) on each half of the pair. So you have two sets of instructions for everything.

Female

Male

WINNING GENES

Most features are a mix of both sets of genes. But in some cases, a weaker or "recessive" gene always gives way to a stronger "dominant" gene. Blue eyes are recessive genes; brown eyes are dominant. So if you have got one brown eye gene, you'll certainly have brown eyes. If both your genes are for blue eyes, though, then your eyes will be blue.

6. GENES MAKE A BODY

Together, the full sequence of genes on all the strands of DNA in all your chromosomes are enough to make all the proteins needed to build your body.

MISSING PARTS

Scientists used to think genes are all there is to the recipe. But you can't make a cake from just a list of ingredients. And it seems you need more than genes to make a body. Just what, scientists don't know yet.

5. CODONS MAKE GENES

Sequences of codons are like sentences, and each sentence is a gene. The words in each sentence give the combination of amino acids needed to build a particular protein.

73

WHAT'S A BOY AND WHAT'S A GIRL?

When you're young, your body works the same way whether you're a girl or boy. You look different, and have different genitals, but you've got the same body systems. This changes when you reach puberty. Puberty is when your reproductive system, the parts of your body that create children, really starts developing.

1. HORMONES AWAY!

It all begins when the hypothalamus sends out the GRH hormone. At once, the nearby pituitary gland reacts by releasing its own hormones: FSH and LH.

Bladder

Testicle

Sperm duct

3. BOY CHANGES

As male sex hormones take effect, a boy grows hair between his legs, under his arms and on his chin. His testes start to make sperm, and by the time he is 15 or so, they make 200 million sperm a day.

THE HORMONES

Six key hormones play a part in the differences between girls and boys. Hormones are chemical messengers that make things happen as they circulate in the blood.

GONADOTROPIN-RELEASING HORMONE (GRH)

FOLLICLE STIMULATING HORMONE (FSH)

LUTEINIZING HORMONE (LH)

TESTOSTERONE

BRAIN HORMONES

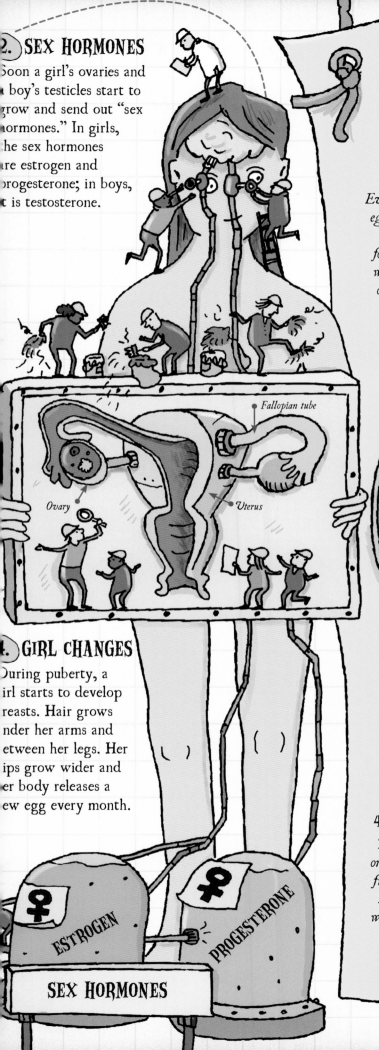

2. SEX HORMONES

Soon a girl's ovaries and a boy's testicles start to grow and send out "sex hormones." In girls, the sex hormones are estrogen and progesterone; in boys, it is testosterone.

Fallopian tube

Ovary

Uterus

4. GIRL CHANGES

During puberty, a girl starts to develop breasts. Hair grows under her arms and between her legs. Her hips grow wider and her body releases a new egg every month.

ESTROGEN

PROGESTERONE

SEX HORMONES

MONTHLY RHYTHMS

After a girl reaches puberty, her body goes through a cycle of changes every 28 days or so. It's called the menstrual cycle and prepares a fresh egg for fertilization.

1. GROWING EGGS

Every girl is born with two egg stores, called ovaries. Here, eggs are held in follicles. The cycle begins when the pituitary sends out FSH, making some follicles start to grow.

2. LINING THE UTERUS

As follicles grow, they release their own hormone, estrogen. Estrogen encourages the lining of the uterus to thicken into a comfy bed for the egg. It also causes the pituitary to send out more LH.

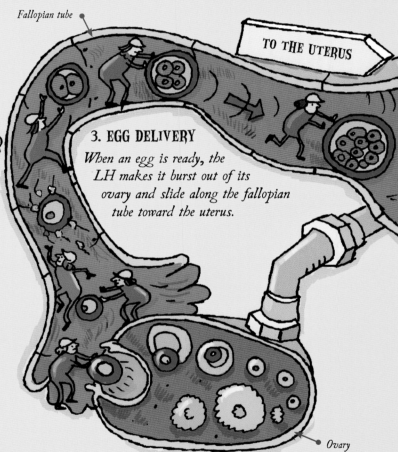

Fallopian tube

TO THE UTERUS

3. EGG DELIVERY

When an egg is ready, the LH makes it burst out of its ovary and slide along the fallopian tube toward the uterus.

Ovary

4. THE OLD FOLLICLE

The abandoned follicle, or "corpus luteum," turns from white to yellow and sends out progesterone, which thickens the uterus lining even more.

5. CYCLE OVER

If the egg is fertilized by a sperm, the process goes further (see next page). If not, the egg and uterus lining are shed when a girl has her period, and the monthly cycle begins again.

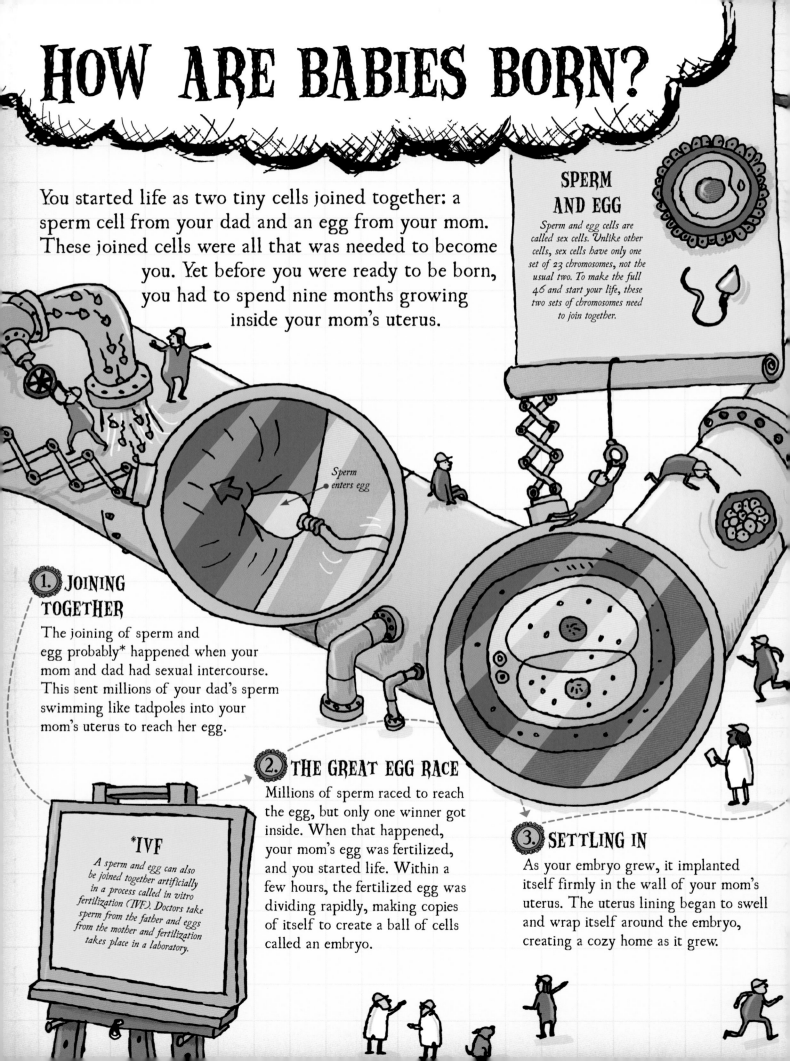

HOW ARE BABIES BORN?

You started life as two tiny cells joined together: a sperm cell from your dad and an egg from your mom. These joined cells were all that was needed to become you. Yet before you were ready to be born, you had to spend nine months growing inside your mom's uterus.

SPERM AND EGG

Sperm and egg cells are called sex cells. Unlike other cells, sex cells have only one set of 23 chromosomes, not the usual two. To make the full 46 and start your life, these two sets of chromosomes need to join together.

Sperm enters egg

1. JOINING TOGETHER

The joining of sperm and egg probably* happened when your mom and dad had sexual intercourse. This sent millions of your dad's sperm swimming like tadpoles into your mom's uterus to reach her egg.

*IVF

A sperm and egg can also be joined together artificially in a process called in vitro fertilization (IVF). Doctors take sperm from the father and eggs from the mother and fertilization takes place in a laboratory.

2. THE GREAT EGG RACE

Millions of sperm raced to reach the egg, but only one winner got inside. When that happened, your mom's egg was fertilized, and you started life. Within a few hours, the fertilized egg was dividing rapidly, making copies of itself to create a ball of cells called an embryo.

3. SETTLING IN

As your embryo grew, it implanted itself firmly in the wall of your mom's uterus. The uterus lining began to swell and wrap itself around the embryo, creating a cozy home as it grew.

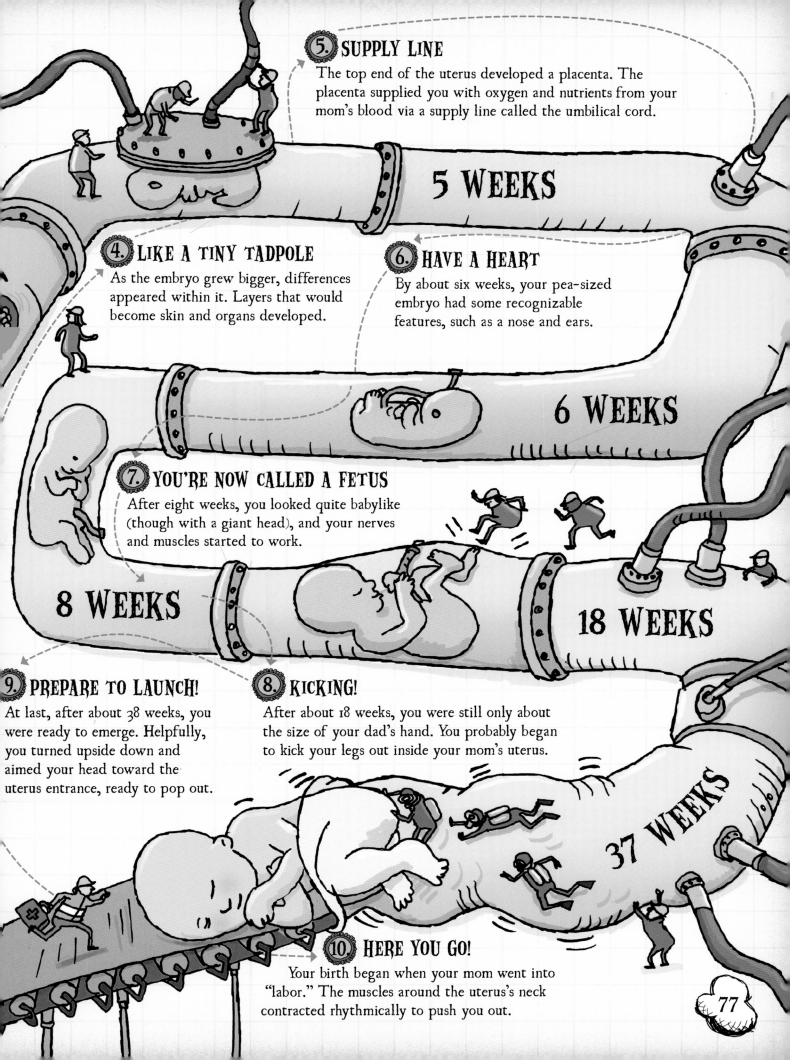

5. SUPPLY LINE

The top end of the uterus developed a placenta. The placenta supplied you with oxygen and nutrients from your mom's blood via a supply line called the umbilical cord.

5 WEEKS

4. LIKE A TINY TADPOLE

As the embryo grew bigger, differences appeared within it. Layers that would become skin and organs developed.

6. HAVE A HEART

By about six weeks, your pea-sized embryo had some recognizable features, such as a nose and ears.

6 WEEKS

7. YOU'RE NOW CALLED A FETUS

After eight weeks, you looked quite babylike (though with a giant head), and your nerves and muscles started to work.

8 WEEKS

18 WEEKS

9. PREPARE TO LAUNCH!

At last, after about 38 weeks, you were ready to emerge. Helpfully, you turned upside down and aimed your head toward the uterus entrance, ready to pop out.

8. KICKING!

After about 18 weeks, you were still only about the size of your dad's hand. You probably began to kick your legs out inside your mom's uterus.

37 WEEKS

10. HERE YOU GO!

Your birth began when your mom went into "labor." The muscles around the uterus's neck contracted rhythmically to push you out.

77

GLOSSARY

Here's a handy guide to some of the tricky words you might find in this book...

adrenaline A hormone sent out by your adrenal glands on top of the kidneys. It helps to boost your body processes in an emergency.

aerobic The normal working of your muscles when they have enough oxygen.

alveolus One of the millions of tiny air sacs in your lungs, which are arranged in clusters shaped like bunches of grapes.

anaerobic When your muscles have to work without oxygen.

antibody One of millions of different proteins that are made by white blood cells, each one of which targets a different germ.

artery A large blood vessel that takes blood away from the heart.

atrium One of the upper spaces in your heart where blood is held before entering the ventricles.

bacteria Tiny microbes. Most are harmless, but there are a few that can make you ill.

blood transfusion The transfer of blood from one person, known as a donor, to another. The donated blood is given to someone with the same blood type.

capillary A microscopically tiny blood vessel that transfers substances between blood and the body's cells.

carbohydrate A part of food that your body converts into glucose to provide energy.

cardiovascular system Your heart and blood circulation, which keeps your body cells supplied with oxygen and food, and which helps to defend your body against germs.

cartilage The tough but stretchy material that protects the ends of your bones and gives shape to some parts of your body, such as your nose and ears.

cell One of the trillions of tiny basic units from which your body is built up.

chyme The sloppy fluid that your stomach turns food into and sends along your gut for digestion.

cilia Microscopic hairlike structures. Millions of these line some of your body's surfaces, such as your airways, and wave to move things along.

circulation The movement of blood around your body.

collagen The tough material that binds parts of your body together.

connective tissue The tissue that holds bones and all the other tissues in your body together.

cytoplasm The material that makes up the inside of every cell. It is made of a fluid filled with lots of tiny structures.

diaphragm A sheet of muscle that forms a dome shape beneath your lungs.

digestive system The long tube that runs through your body from the mouth to the anus. Its job is to break down the food you eat into chemicals your body can absorb and use for various processes.

DNA Short for deoxyribonucleic acid, this is a very long and complex chemical molecule that is found inside every living cell. It provides a complete program for life.

embryo The name for a developing baby up to the eighth week of pregnancy.

endocrine system The system of glands that release chemical hormones into your blood to control how your body works.

enzyme A protein that speeds up chemical reactions in your body.

fetus The name for a developing baby after the eighth week of pregnancy.

gene Part of the DNA that is responsible for providing instructions to make a particular protein.

glucose The simplest kind of sugar, which your body uses as its prime energy source.

hemoglobin An iron-containing protein in every red blood cell, which grabs hold of oxygen for its journey to your body's cells.

hormone A chemical messenger released by glands that circulates in your blood to tell body cells what to do.

immune system The body's clever and varied array of defenses against germs, including white blood cells and antibodies.

leukocyte Another name for a white blood cell.

lymphatic system A network of tubes that carries a liquid called lymph. It plays a role in both the circulatory and immune systems.

lymphocyte The name for a range of white blood cells that fight germs. They include B lymphocytes, T lymphocytes and T killers.

mitochondrion One of the tiny powerhouses found in every cell. They generate energy from sugar and oxygen.

nervous system Your body's messaging system, including the brain, spinal cord and nerves. It carries information from sensors around the body to the brain and sends messages to different body parts telling them how to behave.

neuron A nerve cell.

neurotransmitter A chemical that takes a signal from one nerve cell to another across the gap between them, which is called a synapse.

organ One of the special arrangements of tissues in your body that performs a particular task, such as your heart and liver.

osteocyte A specialized type of bone-making cell.

oxygen The gas in the air that every cell in your body needs for releasing energy from glucose.

protein The main building material in your body, and an essential part of your diet.

pulse The rhythmic throbbing sent through your blood as your heart pumps.

red blood cell One of the 20–30 trillion cells in your blood that carry oxygen, turning bright red as they do so.

respiratory system Your breathing system, including your lungs and airways, which takes oxygen from the air into the body and gets rid of unwanted carbon dioxide.

RNA A temporary form of DNA used for everyday working.

sarcomere One of the tiny power units that make up muscle tissue.

skeletal muscle The muscle tissue that forms the muscles attached to your skeleton, which enable you to move.

skeleton Your body's framework of bones.

smooth muscle The muscle tissue that forms tubes and bags inside your body. Smooth muscle is found in your gut where it pushes food along and in your blood vessels where it controls blood flow.

striated muscle Another name for skeletal muscle. Striated muscles are formed of rows of muscle fibers, giving them a striped or striated appearance.

synapse The tiny gap between neighboring nerve cells.

tissue The basic materials from which your body is made. Tissues are built of similar cells.

urinary system The system that keeps your body's water levels nearly constant, and removes excess as urine. It also removes some waste products from your body. The system includes your kidneys and bladder.

vein One of the large blood vessels that carry blood back to the heart.

ventricle One of the lower chambers in your heart that squeeze to pump blood around your body.

virus A tiny microorganism that only comes to life once it has invaded and taken over a living cell, such as one of your body cells.

white blood cell The name given to a wide range of cells in the immune system. These circulate in your blood, defending your body against germs.

INDEX